Appu Jasu

The Poetics of a Line

KERBER PHOTO ART

preface

One cannot talk about the moment, the prefix, or the process of turning out without unnecessarily accumulating distance. Nothing the story might do can't help the evaporating that will occur as the objects try to take foot. The former is transmutation by giving, latter a forced offering that has to fill the other half. To abstain from forming the question is to enclose all existence in only one's absolute. To abstain from addressing the question is to become a part of the inanimate.

About the inanimate: the existence of stagnating objects, stones, bits, pieces and grains is again a history impossible to be told, a reality that is nothing but a closed construction of mirrors, a still vortex, and there is nothing in a mirror until a movement emerges, and if it stops only an active memory can keep it alive.

As the weightless body floats among the mirrors it is indifferent whether the surfaces are hollow or solid, the reflections will reach new grounds as far as the body flows. It is only another motion within the fields that can alter the direction of the body's trajectory in space, forcing it to curve, bringing forth the figure beginning to draw: a creation substantially distinct from a reflection.

The difference of existence and nonexistence is almost next to nothing, as nonexistence is only the negative of a being and thus a clear diverging from nothingness, yet still compared to existence a totally different condition of being. This negative is however never a creation of anything new, but only the dim image of existence, petrified and limited within the original's route. Once confronted, the existent is destabilized by the image of the nonexistent, or is transilluminated by the light of its negative colors.

Nonexistence is possible only after existence, and only with it. "(Community) – in every public or private exchange of words, makes the final silence resound, the silence where, however, it is never certain that everything comes, finally, to an end. No end there where finitude reigns."[o]

The movement is curious and driven by uncertainty. The sense and logic of the initial reaction will remain inscribed within the fabric of the act itself, its proportion however always diminishing as the amount of figures multiply. Numbness is not counteraction against the core fright nor estranging from an earlier movement, but difficulty in calibrating the locus of the movement, or seeing the core too clearly.

The only closed circuit that can be found is between the existent and the nonexistent, and there too the nonexistent only follows. Where impulses keep propagating, visions remain symbols constantly rearranging. The spirit of motion is embodied within the forms and actions arising from the spine of every being, the only thing that lodges is the everlasting branching; following it backwards can only be a flash traversing the nerve tracks. Every forming picture will be cut open by the words that it inhabits. To propose a natural is to institute limits. Nothing can start from nothingness, but then again change is only bound to nothingness: beginnings and endings are agreements, notions, and thus only as little real as everything else and as much real as everything else.

1

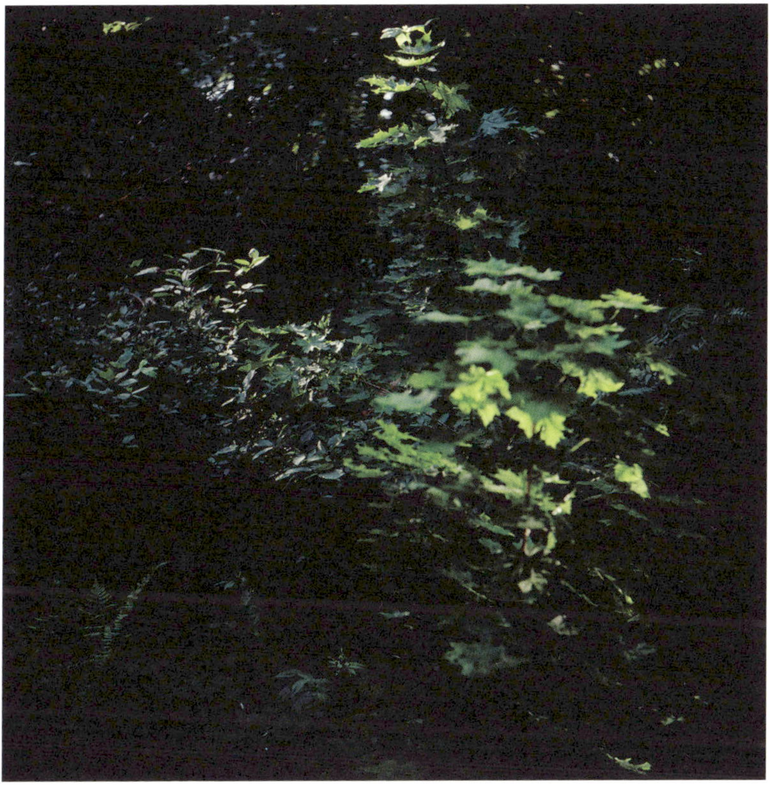

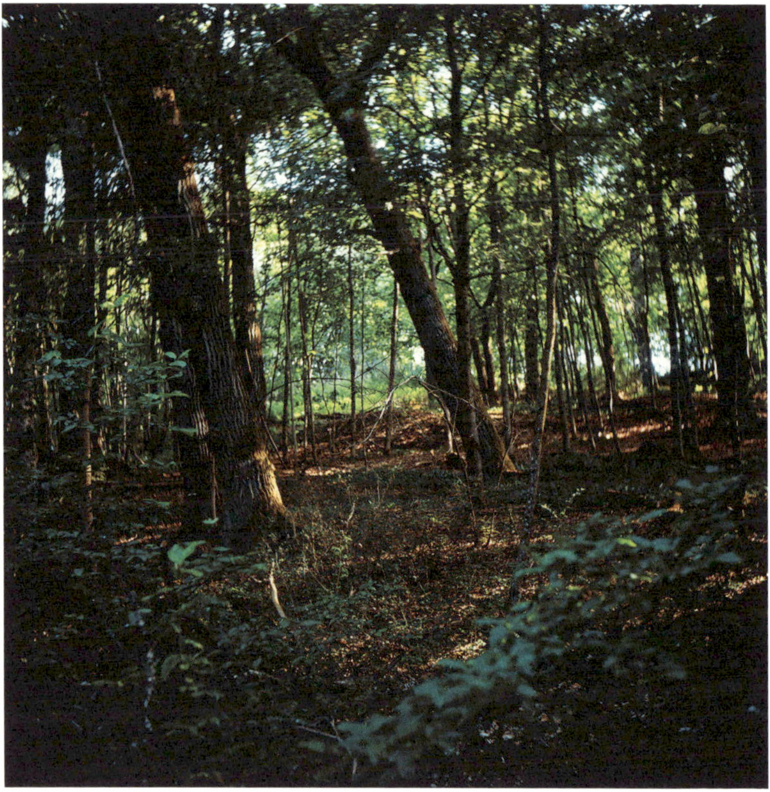

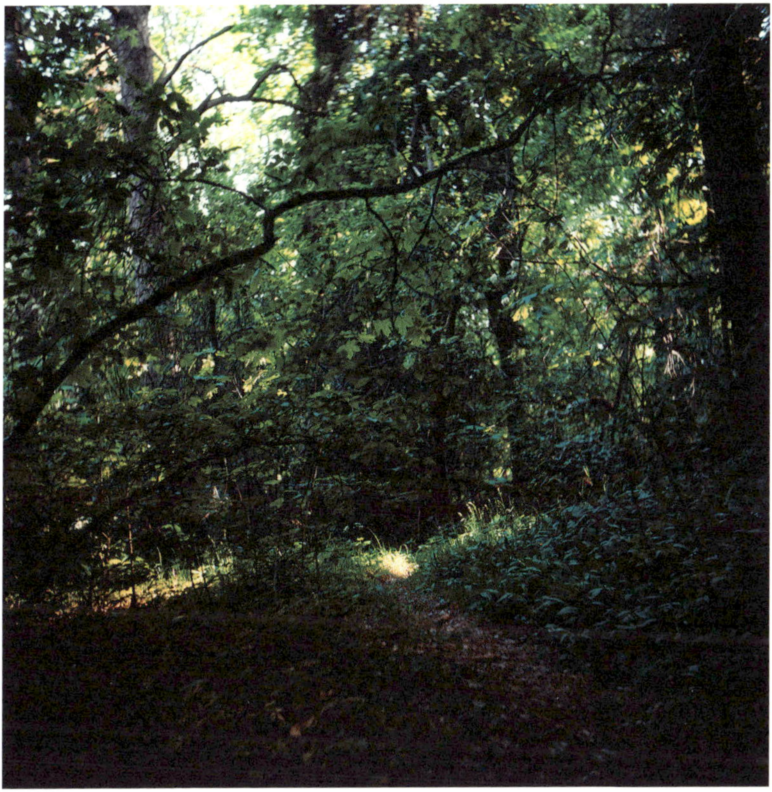

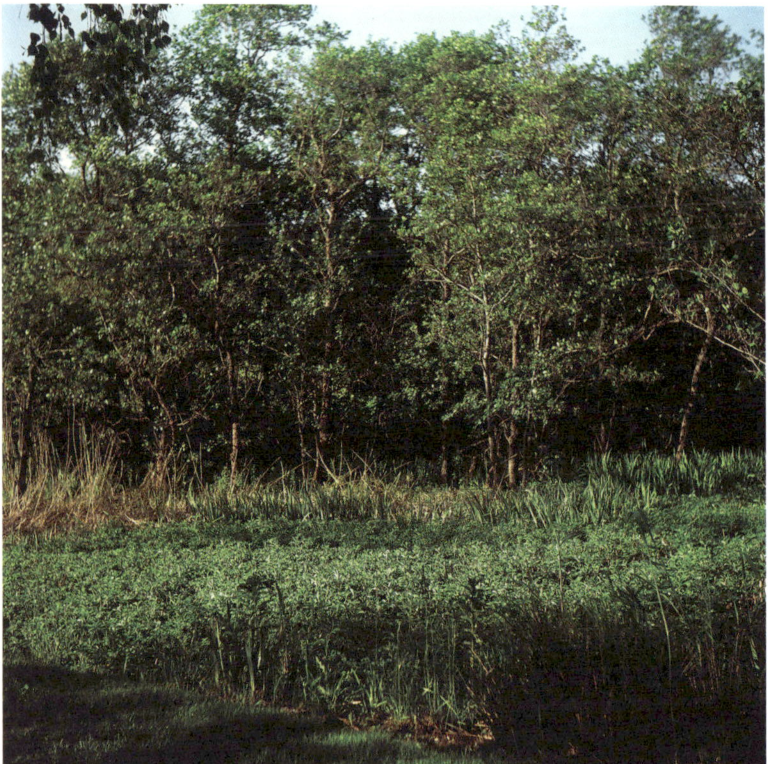

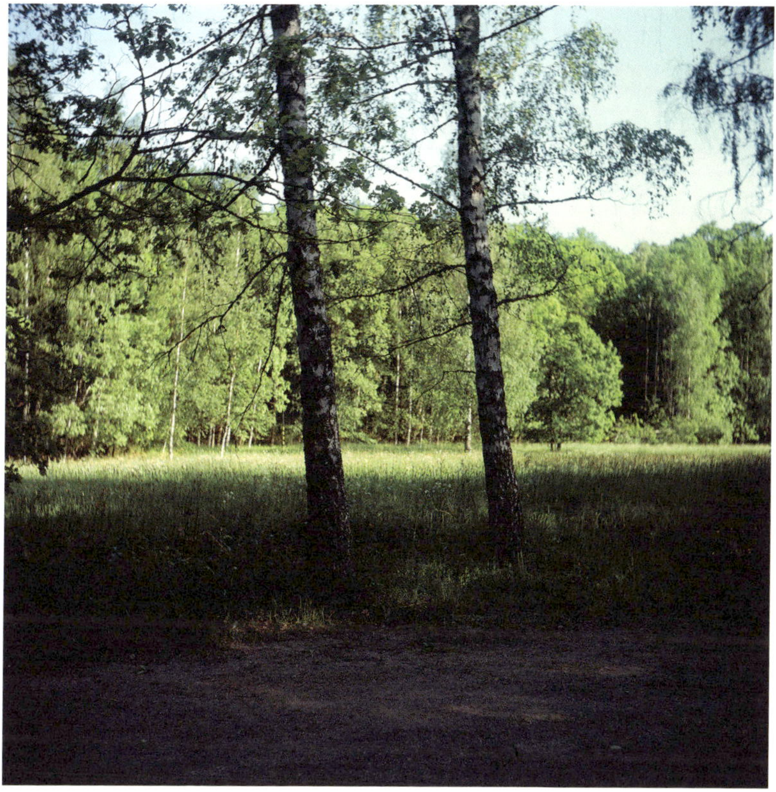

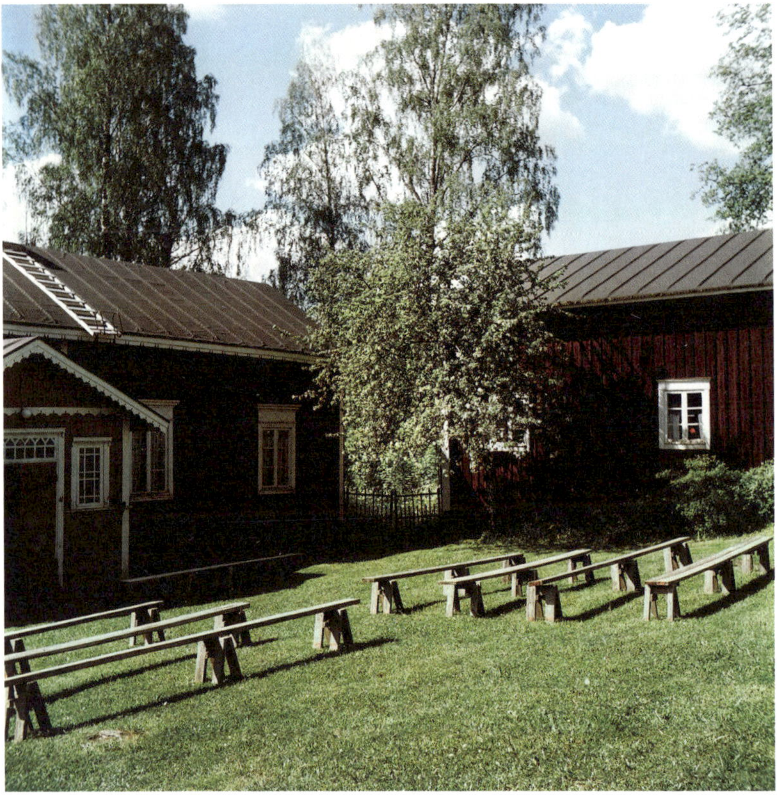

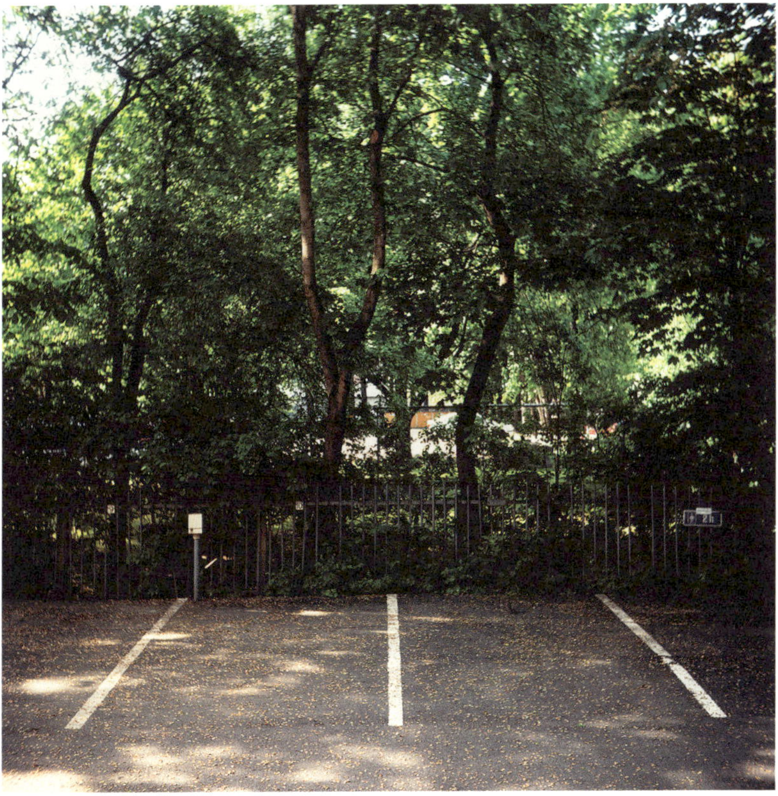

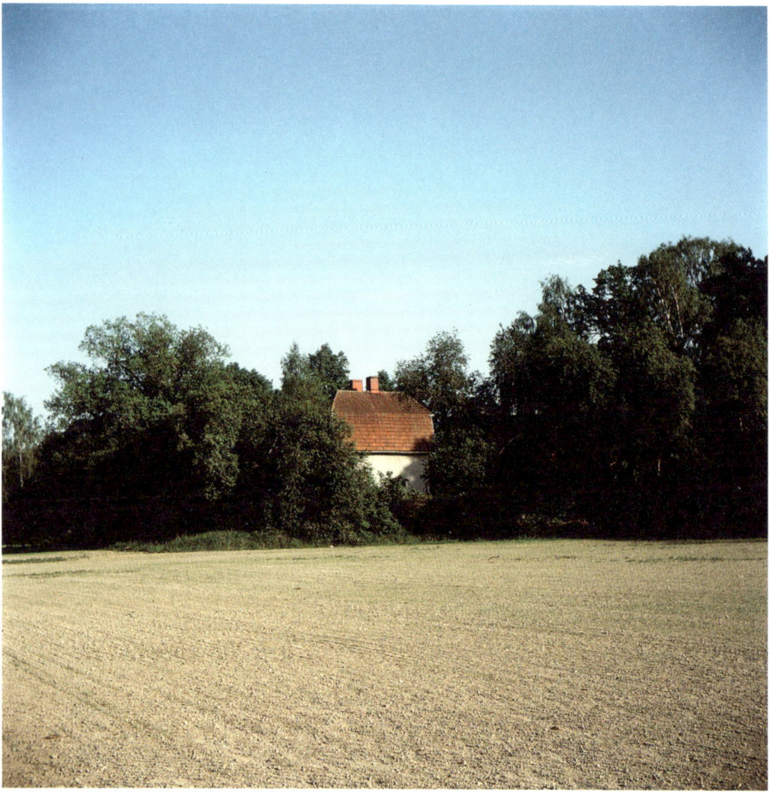

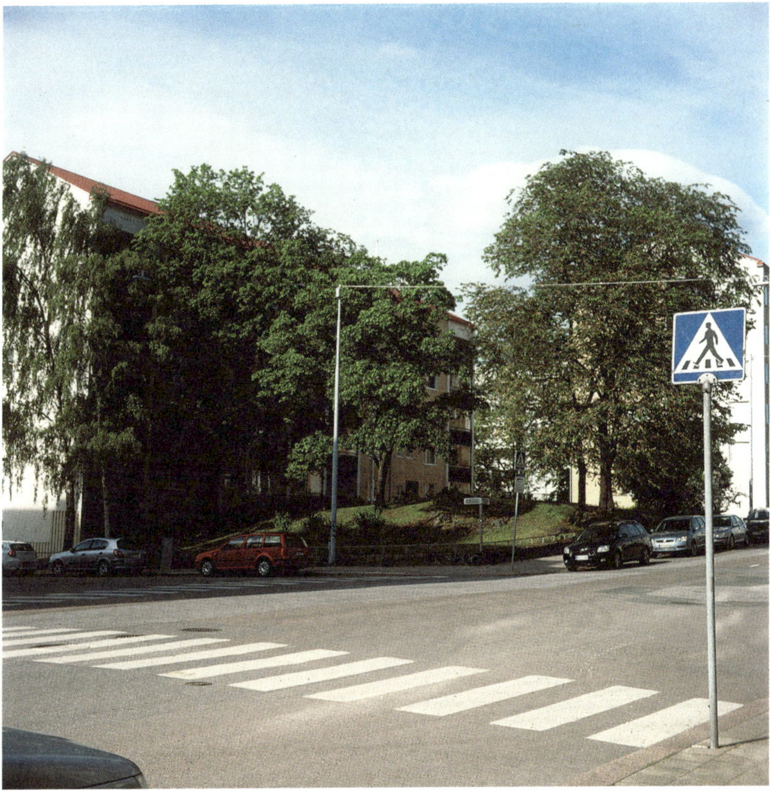

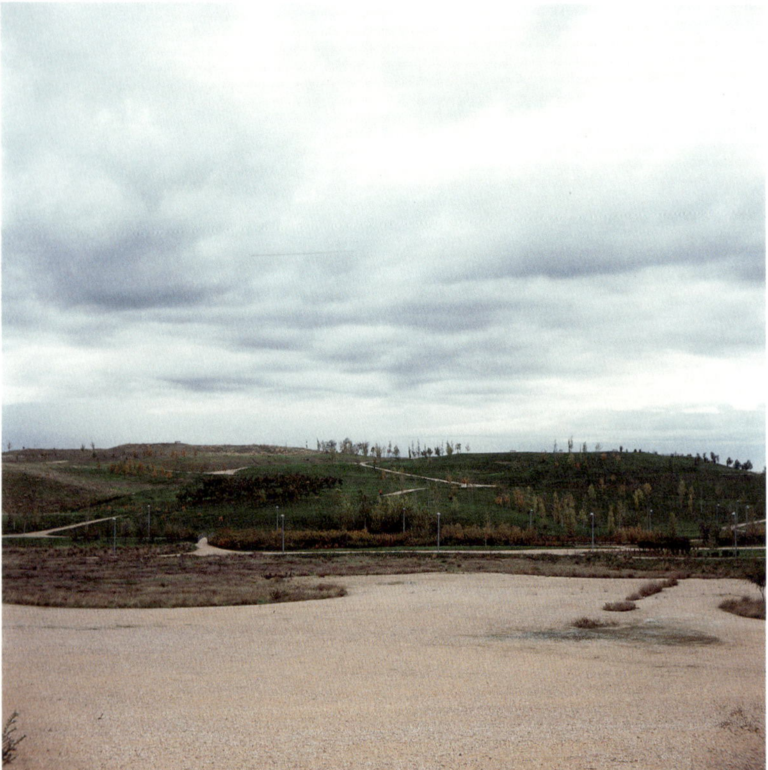

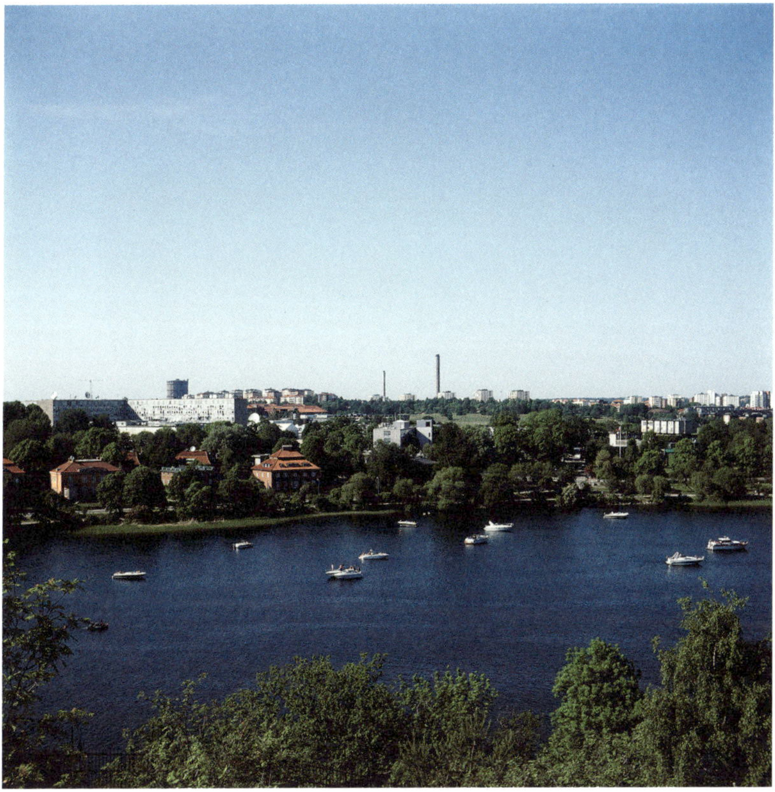

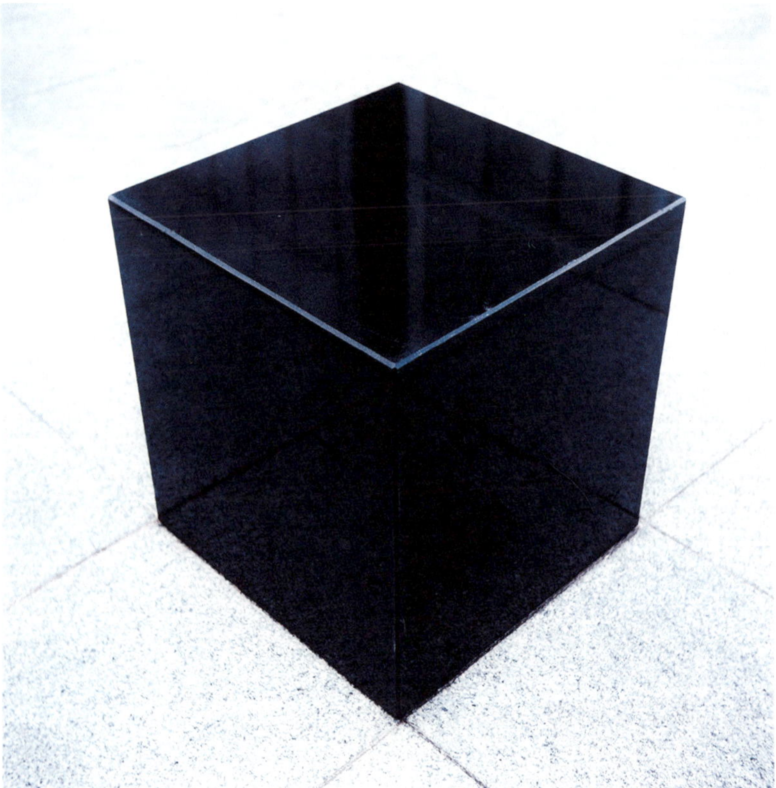

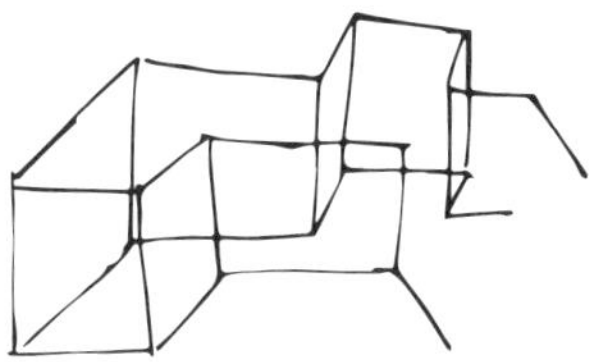

What presence

a. A line appears in between of two points. Noticing them or thinking of them is enough to form the connection.

b. Every possibility that can be conceived is included within the line, but often only a small fraction of them become visible, even in the realm of imagination.

c. On the other hand the line itself is only a small part of a greater whole, and within that might not even be that central.

d. Its direction of movement is not only between points A and B but it ripples into other dimensions also.

e. The line is never realized. While it unobstructedly keeps appearing, it is at the same time always broken and interrupted, not meant to be a fixed and closed chain, and it is in this nonexistence and incompleteness that its presence and suspense resides.

f. The points entail their own gravity that accelerates as they get closer to each other.

g. Because of that they can fully reach each other only if they for some reason or another first drift into mutual proximity.

h. A complicated line can make the equation of the points seem impossible, but that does not mean that it doesn't have a possible solution.

i. When viewed from afar the figure looks completely abstract, from close it can be imagined to contain some logic, but its future is present only as pieces divided into multiple dreams.

j. As it strengthens the line builds up around itself, surrounded with threads that circle it.

k. The line can come apart gradually, partially, unnoticed, intentionally, from the inside, only from the outside, unexpectedly. In the most extreme occasion it seems to break completely and the ends start to drift apart; as to fill the appearing space we return back to section a.

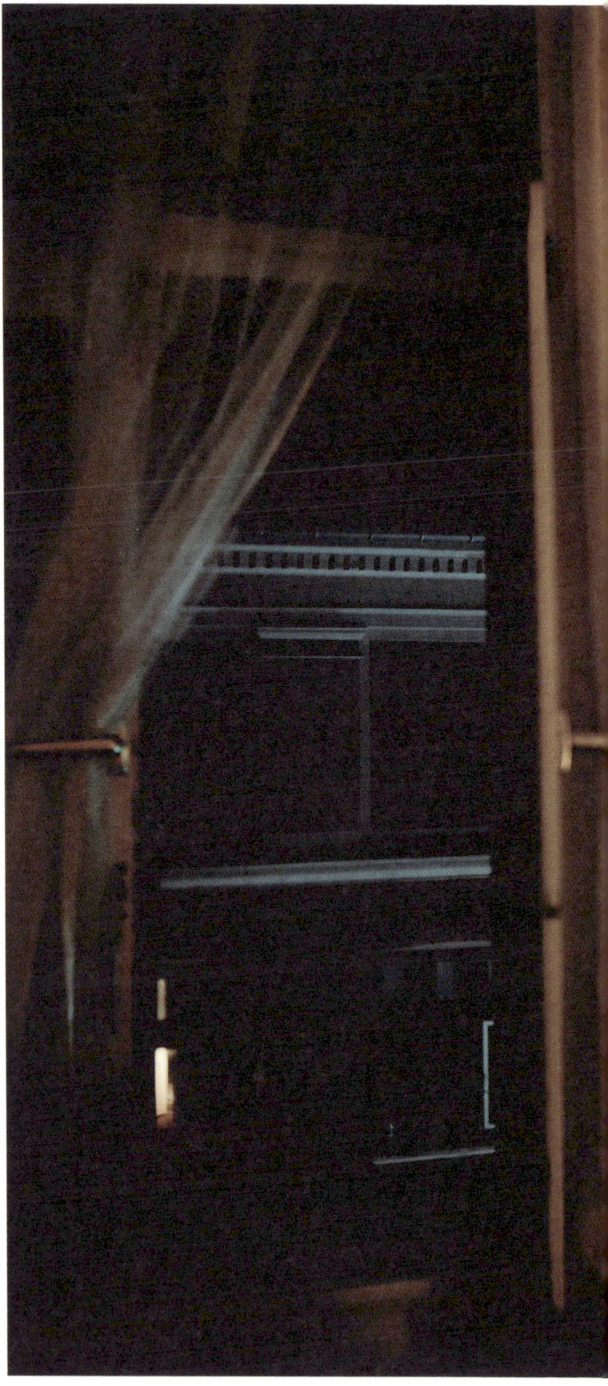

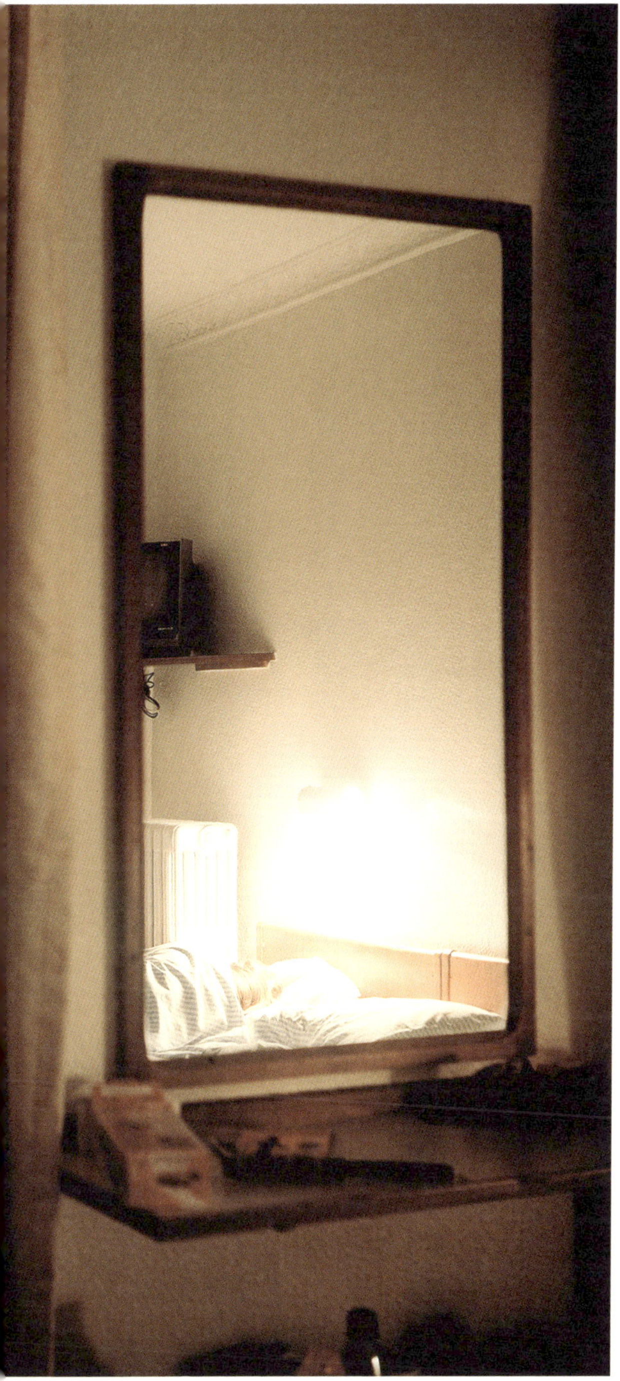

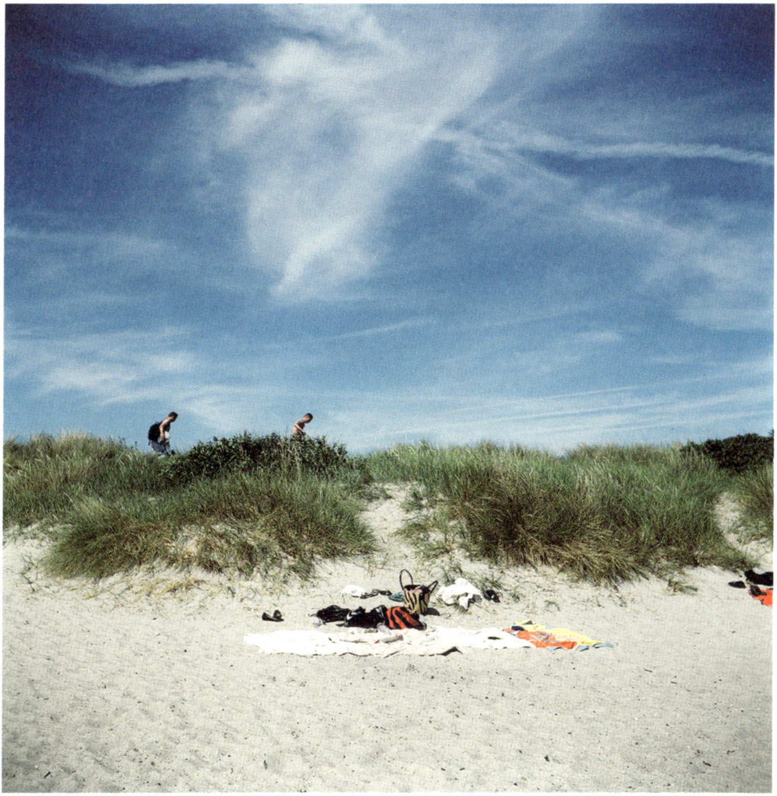

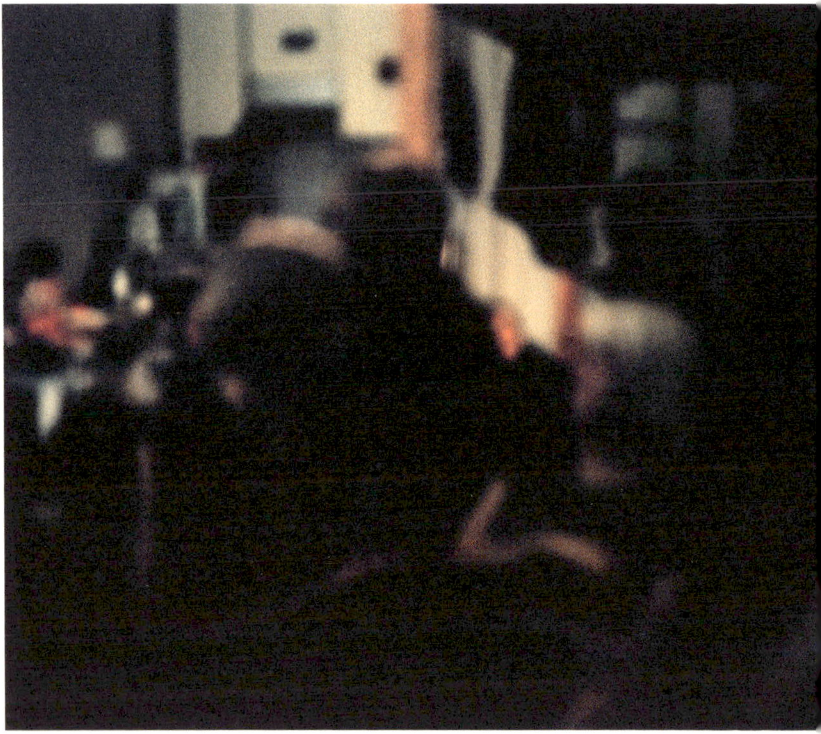

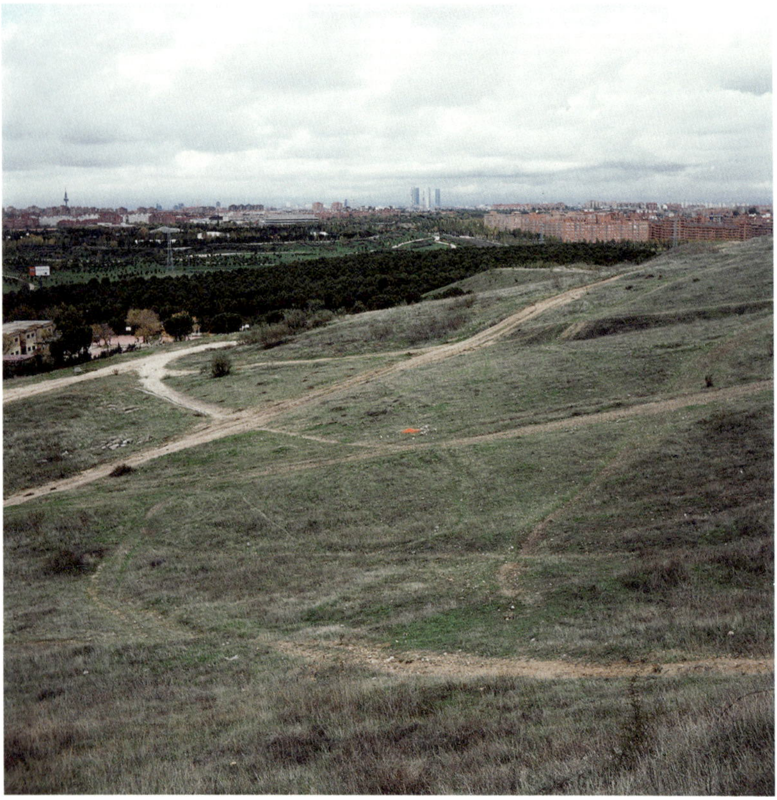

trace

Trace is a result of two lines intersecting. It is a reclining memory of movement, time, thought, gravity, light, humidity. The temporal duration of the trace depends on the natures of both the original incident and the ones following it.

sign

Intentional fabrication of a sign is a way to transfer part of the fabric envisioned by the inner weave into a universe that is perceivable by other agents. As it shifts into another space the sign faces a group of new connections, whereupon its core divides into many parts.

meaning

Take with. Larger signs are even more dense figurations of the map formed by points and lines, although here a map is an overly straightforward concept where the movement would be a concrete transition from one place to another (maps are continuous in expiring). According to Maurice Merleau-Ponty the covert line in paintings contain by way of vibration or radiation a movement that does not lead to displacement.[14]

diffusion

The relationship of mind and signs, of the being and space is complex and unstable: a connection defined by terms and transactions with constant proposals and rectifications. The mind composes thoughts as spaces, the mere passing of time requires them to align spatially. The mind seeks a connection with the outer space by identifying. Aspiration is to find unities between mind and signs.

structure

With each relation the dimensions of space and the dimensions of line get more and more fine-tuned. Accumulation happens often intentionally, but also in circumstances that limit the will and possibilities significantly.

milieu

The physical and mental beings of people usually move in spaces that are heavily planned and even controlled. These spaces are results of a long lasting determination and power struggle of points and lines. Countless amounts of both are needed to complete a small house, not to mention a tower block or a whole infrastructure; thought, concept, theory, misconception. Whether the lines are skiis or a cage depends on their fluidity: the lines have a live meaning only when they make new connections possible, otherwise it is a museum meant to retain power by force.

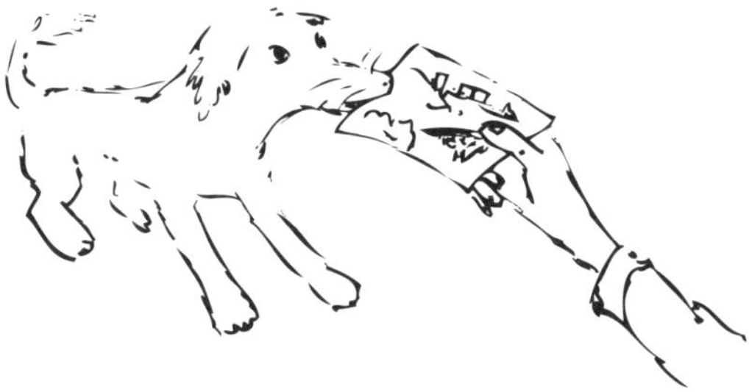

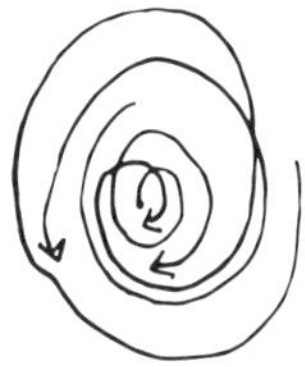

"the undetermined unity of all the faculties"[15]

As the bundle of rays gets tangled into a multifaceted and omnidirectional group, the recurring and intersecting laps in its way start to mount up to a reflective surface where the collateral proposals rise and fall. This accumulating resource of instances starts to either dissect both the forthcoming and already collected apparitions, or averts the unknown and lets the familiar go through.

If selected, the anatomizing of accrual and future lines dissolves the division made into an inside and an outside, as analyzing continuously brings forth new impulses which originate neither in the subject nor the object – they are not born by filiation, and attach themselves loosely both around and across the earlier clustered lines. The core shifts towards the outlines, which are turning into a kind of ascending hum.

Endeavor #1

Above all the connections arise from the effect of time. Time exposes to movement, it denies everything that seeks permanence but is the requirement of all existence.

Time collects moments into a continuum that breaks and overlaps itself. On the following spread there is a painting, and a picture made as an attempt to accumulate a cluster of time:

> A video camera takes the place of the eye wandering over the surface of the painting. After the painting has been watched for a while, the 2028 frames of the video are collected away from the temporal dimension and rearranged as a two-dimensional surface. The length of the watching: 1 min 55 s.

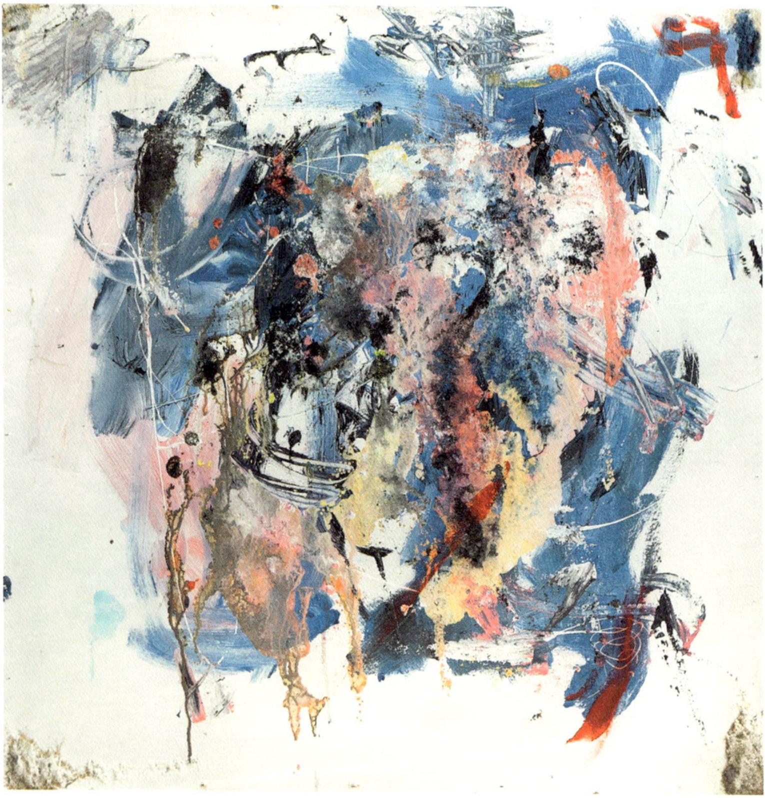

Four Seasons in the Abyss (Winter)
by Timo Marila

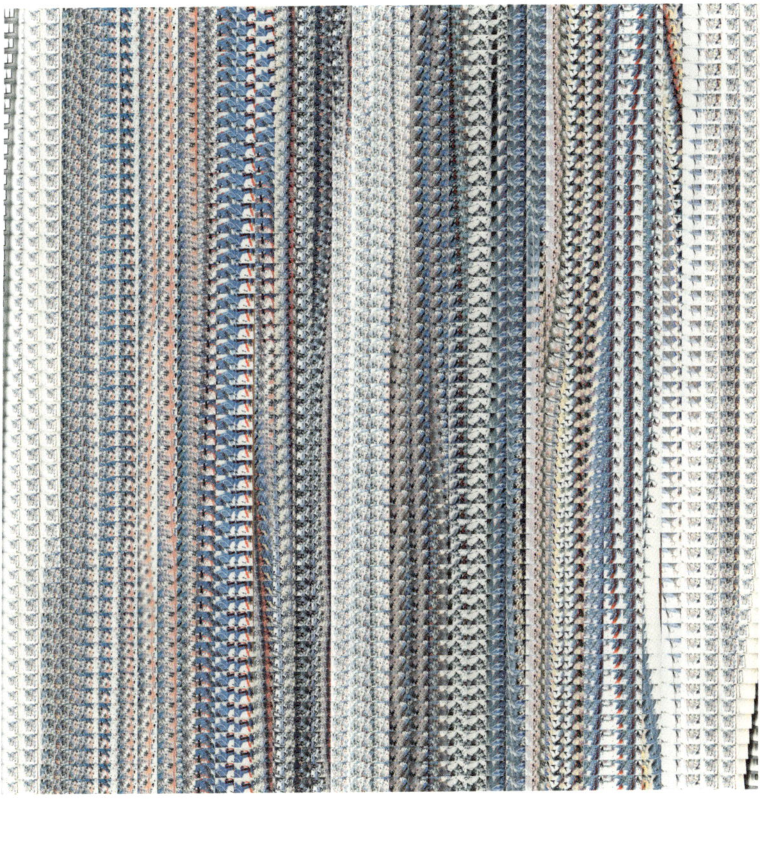

Looking at "Four Seasons in the Abyss (Winter)" by Timo Marila for 1 min 55 s

Endeavor #2

Two and a half years of dating over the sea makes up 75 tickets for one side of the relationship.

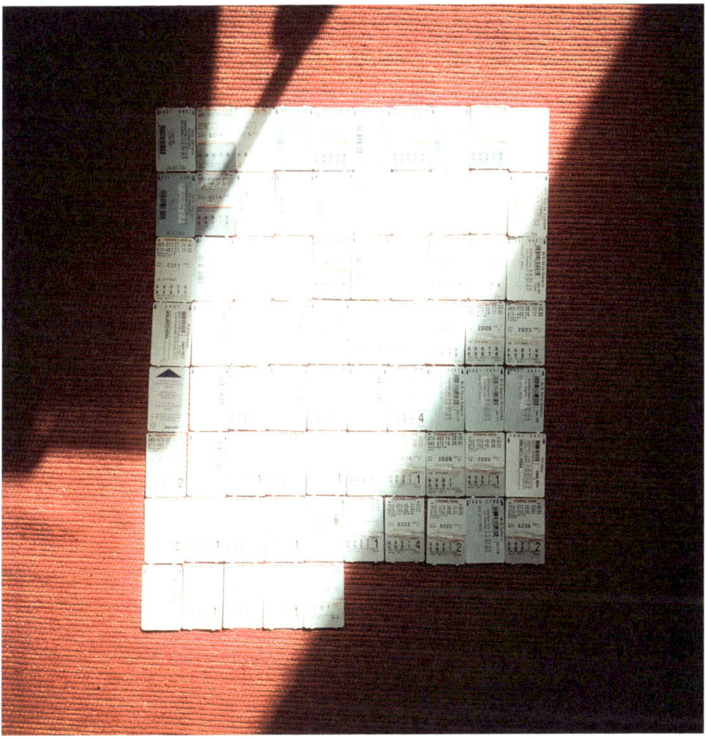

The trip over the bay is usually made with one of the four passenger ships that leave the harbour at nine each morning and night. The duration of the travel is 11 hours one way.

In this figure of one of the ships there is a cross over each cabin the person has slept in during that time (of which in the cabin number 2008 twice, and in cabins number 2002 and 2017 three times).

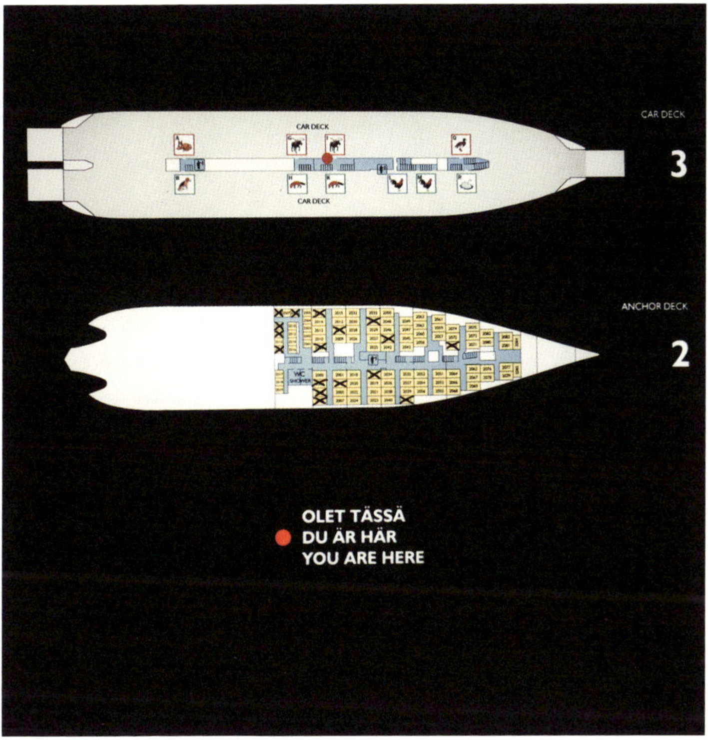

CAR DECK
3
CAR DECK
CAR DECK
ANCHOR DECK
2
WC
SHOWER
OLET TÄSSÄ
DU ÄR HÄR
YOU ARE HERE

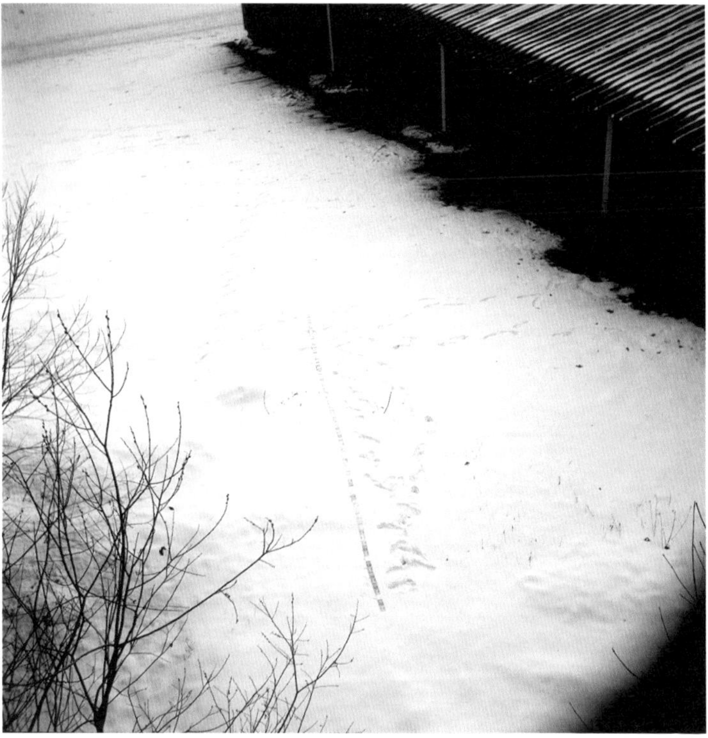

If all the tickets are placed one after another, the length of the line will be 6 meters and 33 centimeters. As the whole line embodies 2,5 years, it can be calculated that one centimeter corresponds to 34 hours. The overall surface area of the cards is 3 378 cm2, so 1 cm2 = 6,4 hours.

This process is really slow when put into the proportions of human life: it would take 250 years to fill up the floor of even a modest-sized one-room apartment.

Endeavor #3

The fabric of visually perceiveable space is made of colors, lights and shades. Colors reflect the light's angle and the rotation of shadows. Seems light flows downwards, worn back into the ground by the shadows, passing throught the reflections.

To be able to visually examine the position the mind takes within the space, one has to collect everything surrounding a point into one. The following photos are taken rotating the camera 360 degrees while keeping the shutter open. Everything around the camera will thus draw in into the picture, and the photo will become a common denominator for the objects in the space, the body of lines.

in a forest (temperate broadleaf, spring) (360° on x-axis)

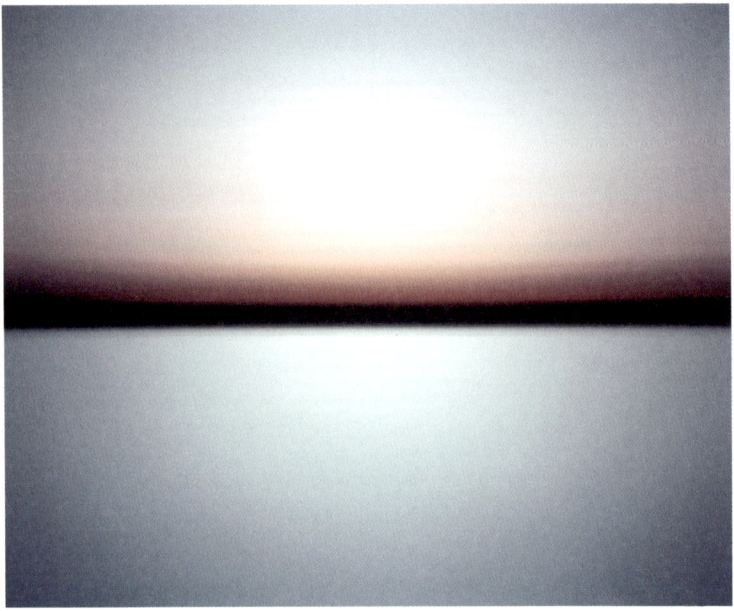

in the middle of a field (winter) (360° on x-axis)

in the middle of a field (autumn) (360° on x-axis)

in a town by a river (360° on y-axis)

in the middle of a field (autumn) (360° on y-axis)

in the backyard after sunset (360° on y-axis)

by a lake, sunset (360° on y-axis)

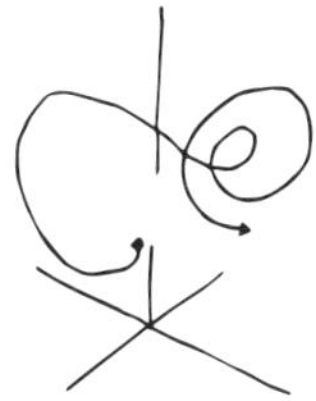

Aperiodic oscillations

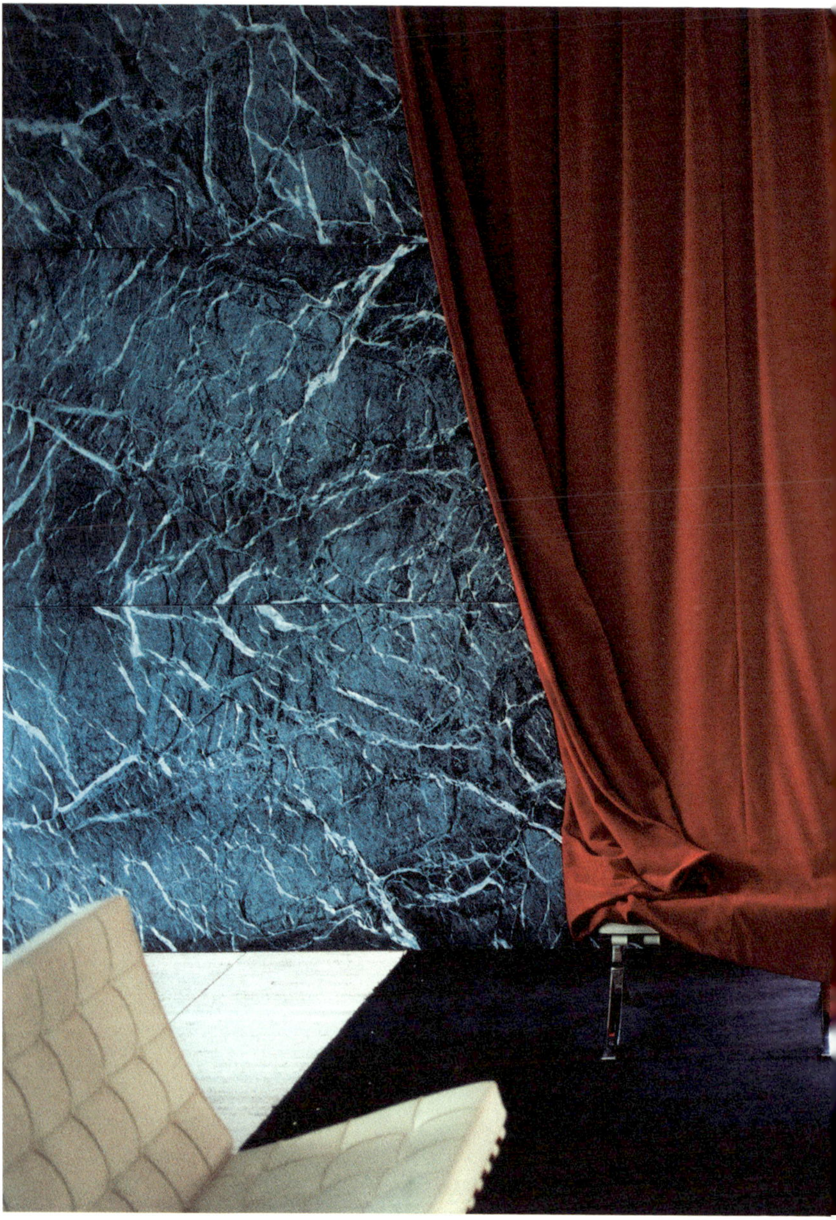

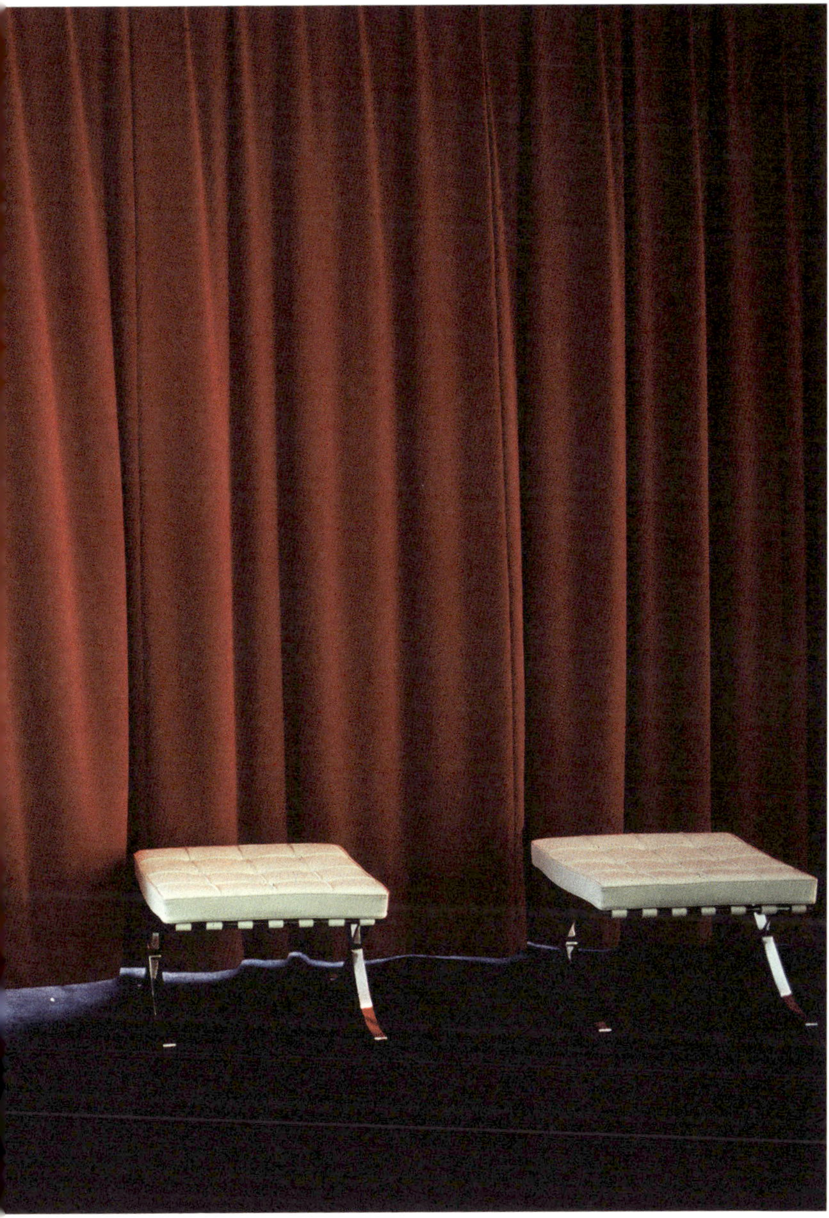

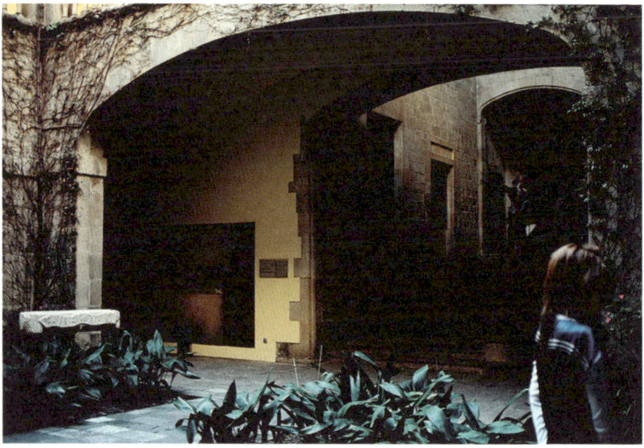

wave

Where the line keeps bending is the wave of sound, tracing the movement that caused it, like an occurring memory that keeps reliving the happened. In a straight line sound disappears into a silence that then awakes the voices of the nonexistent.

In order to advance in space, sound waves need a matter that will act as a mediator. Most common will be air, a substance that the eye sees mainly when it is stuck inside another matter. Sound is not seen even then, but only via meters that mimic its motion. Sound is movement, of which it is itself also a sign of.

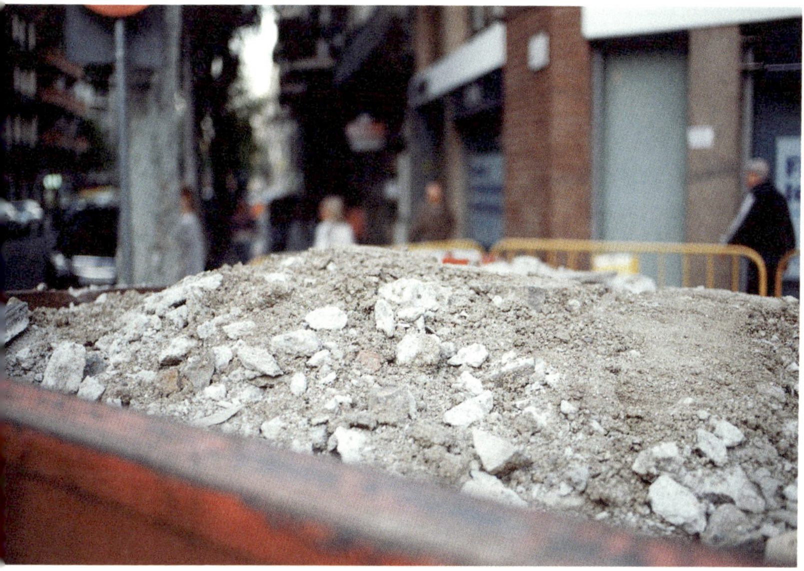

echo

Frequency determines the length of the wave with the speed of its movement. When sound encounters a physical matter, part of it will spring back from it, and an accumulation of conjoined reflections results to a reverberation; history is already present in the sound as it arrives.

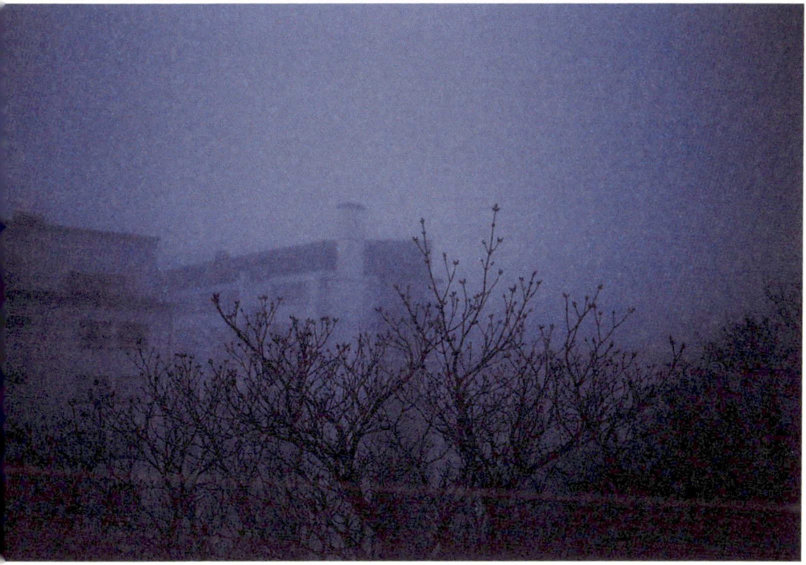

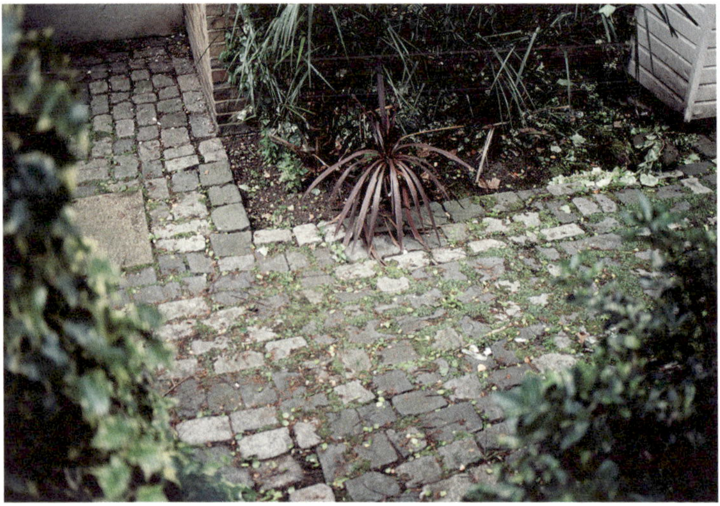

music

Music is said to be the only art form besides architecture to completely surround a person. A person senses the direction of voices three-dimensionally, but the music itself also opens into new dimensions from which its space is composed of. This space is where the listeners meet when they hear music being played from the same source, or a place both have access to and a connection with.

notation

To signal the notes that form a composition, points are drawn on the staff (a set of lines on a paper). Points may have another line attached to them, depending on the duration of the note – the length of its ringing time. Music too unfolds most notably in the temporal dimension, the lines filled with points continue page after page.

note

A voice circles the note like it is standing still, yet it only exists in motion. The sound quivers around the point, at the tense but unattainable presence of its notion. Two voices sounding at the same time create a harmony: the space between two or more notes moving at different frequencies forming converging figures with their overlapping waveforms.

harmony

Harmony originates in the Greek word *harmos* for "joint", related to "arm". The encounter happens in physical space, but the concept of harmony, the connection between them comes into existence in the mind that repeats their place in time and space, their height, loudness, tone and timbre.

sound

Sound is strictly connected to the moment when it happens. Like light, it is pure energy that continues to traverse until it is divided into countless number of parts. Eugène Minkowski has used sound as an allegory describing the dynamic origin of life. In his tableau, the voice is an element that breaths everything into life, sounding the leaves in the trees throughout the whole forest. In this image voice fills life as if it was closed in a vase, echoing back and forth from its every point.[16] But I'm thinking, even vases have an opening?

voice

Light is more or less always based on the percussions of the earth's nearest fiery globe called the sun, but sound is local, an intimate application of light, the earth's personal fingerprint. Light calls flora like fauna call themselves.

hearing

Ears, synapses – we have developed the ability to sense sounds – the microscopic cityscapes, galaxies and forests their waveforms both visibly and audibly contain; they link and interfere, color our vision. Filter is a trill in a shape of a hundred nights and myriad streets and years in the comfy chair, a score you can see through; a tune is a scratch that rings out the voices of the ancestors, blue that foresees the tumultuous years.

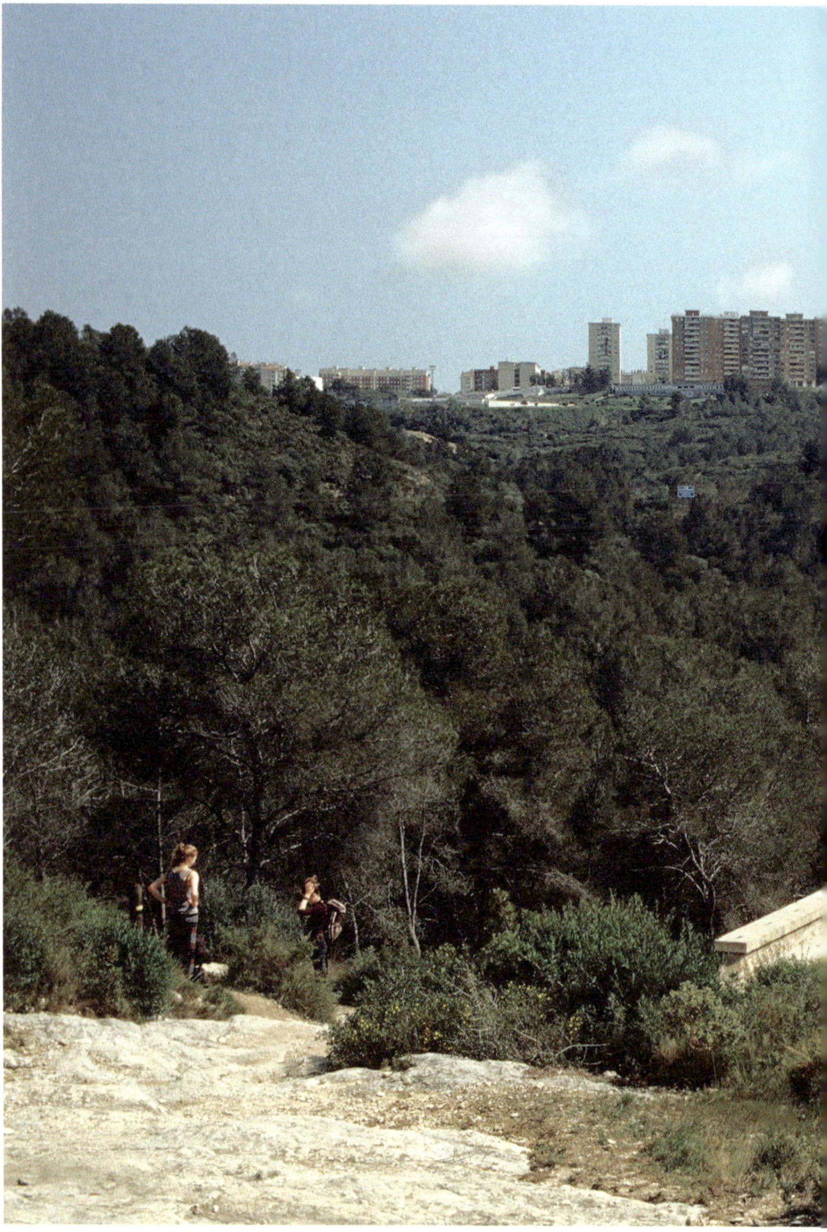

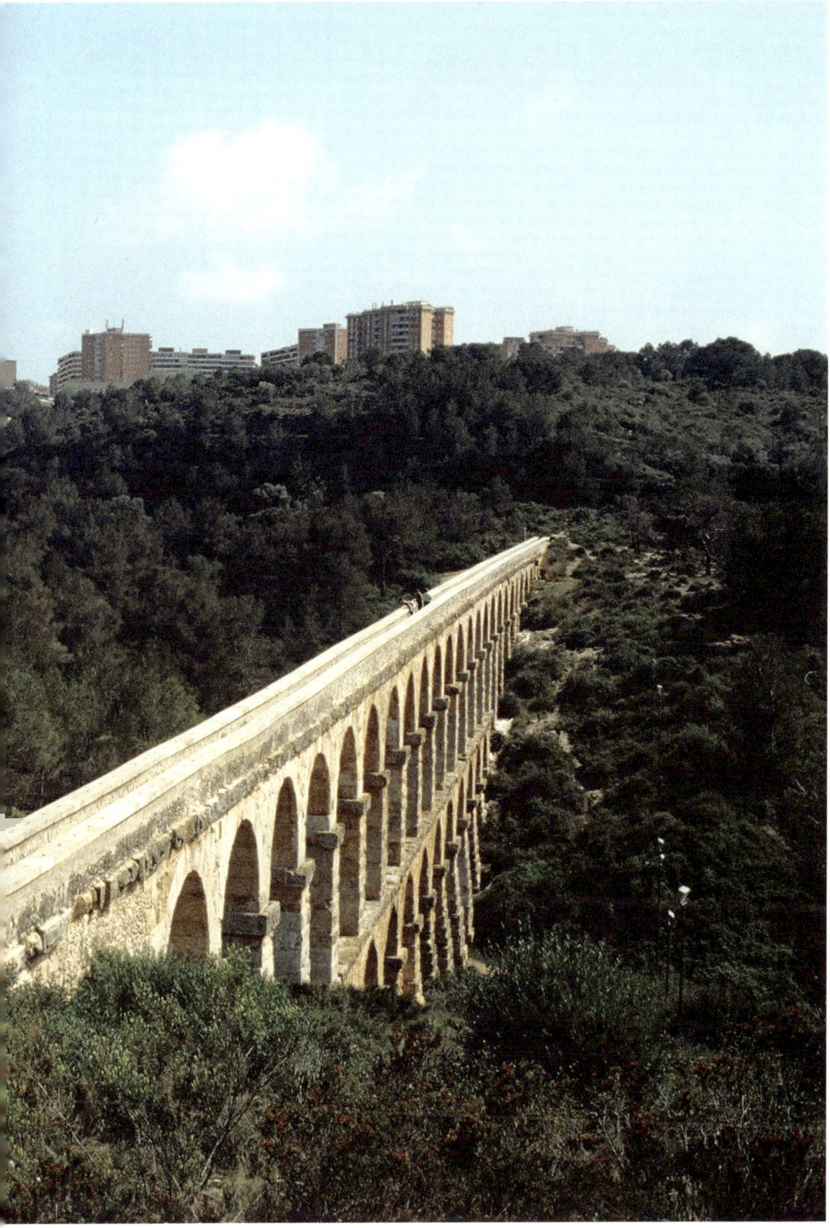

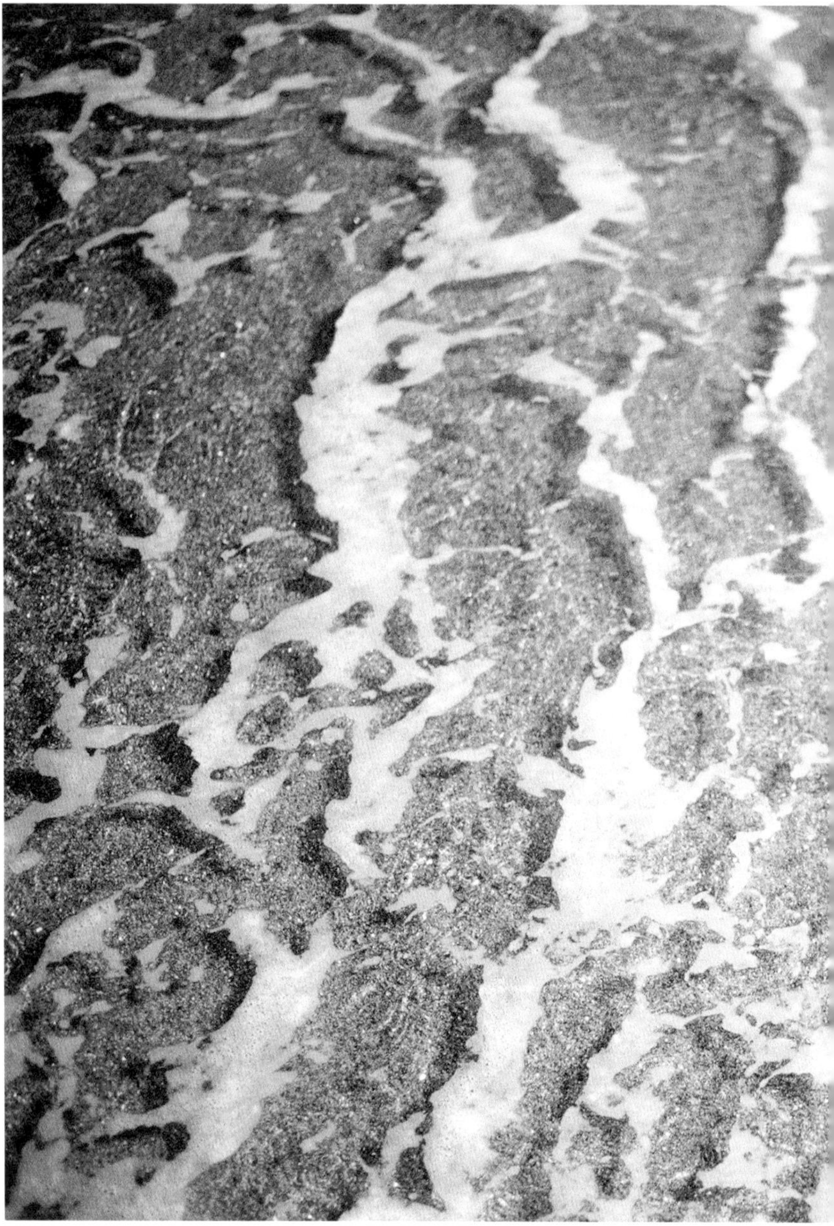

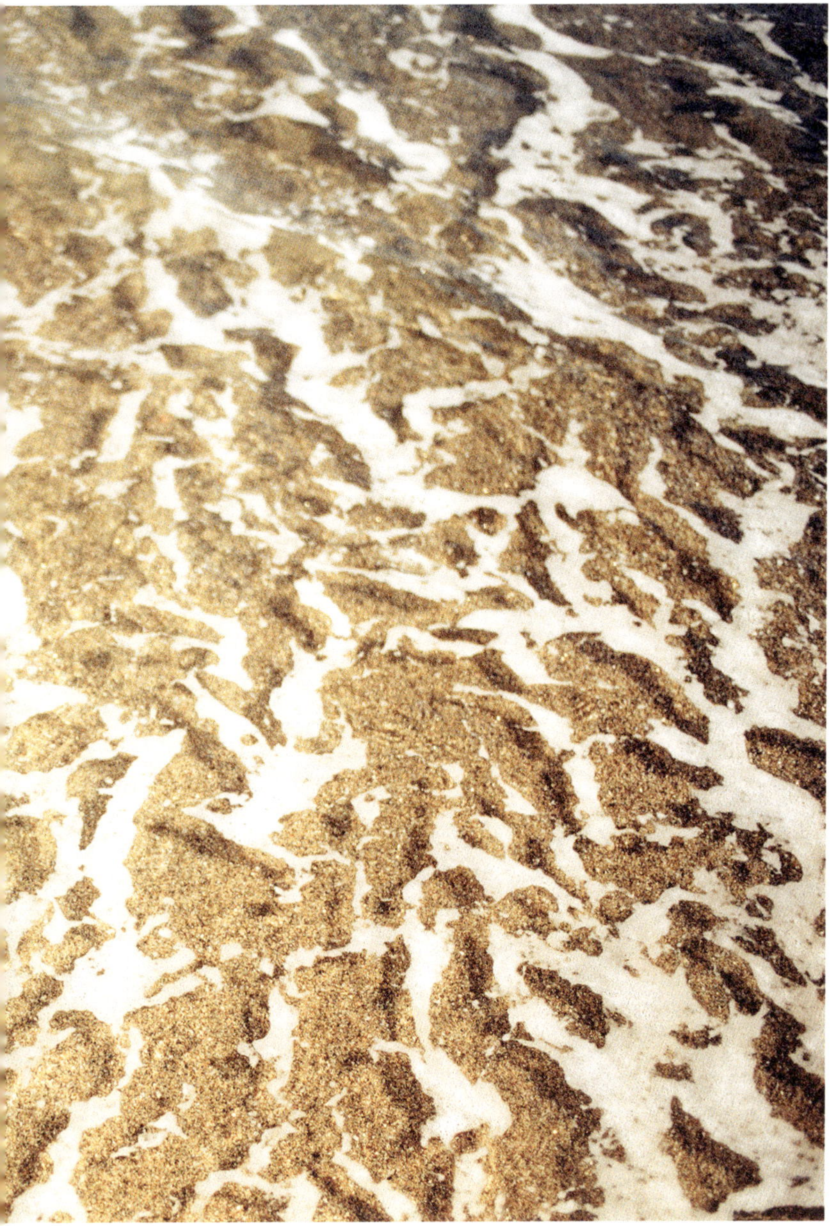

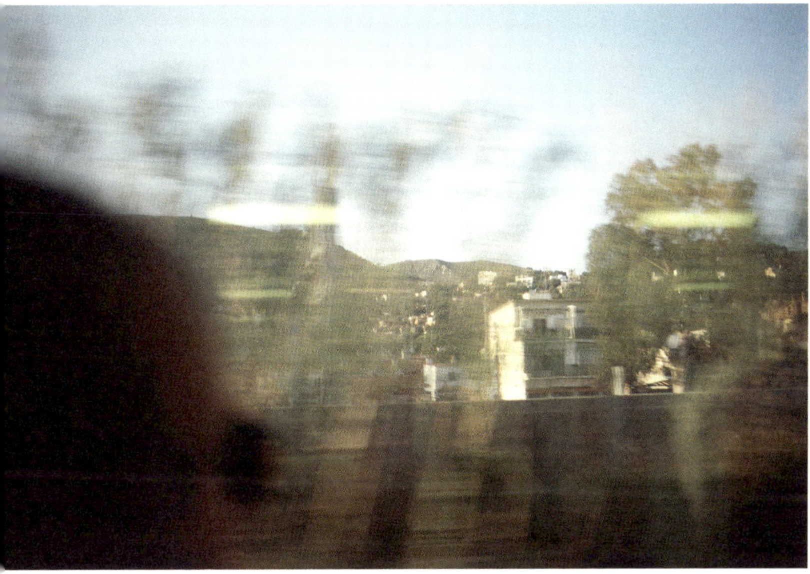

I will keep seeing this again and again, but it will always

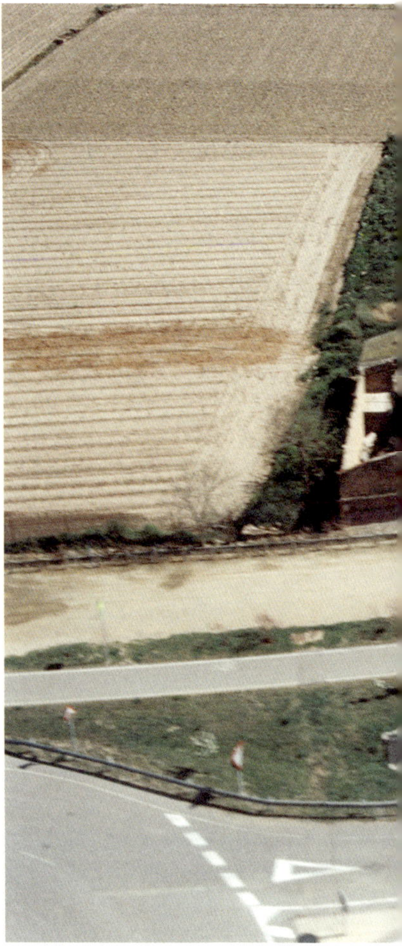

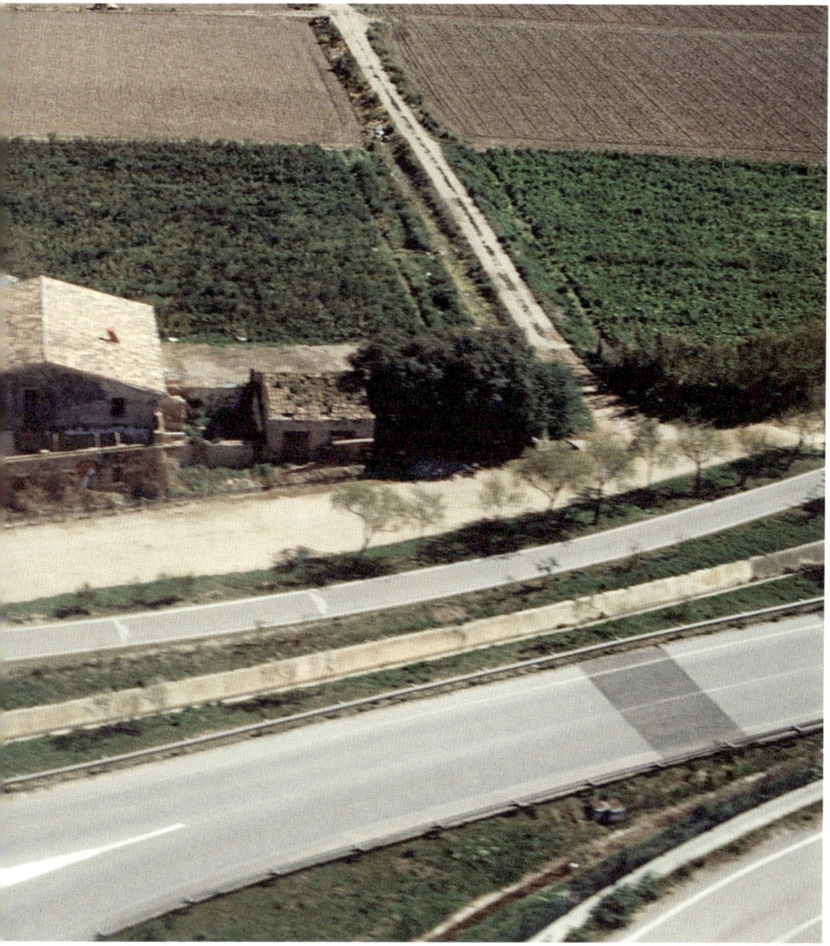

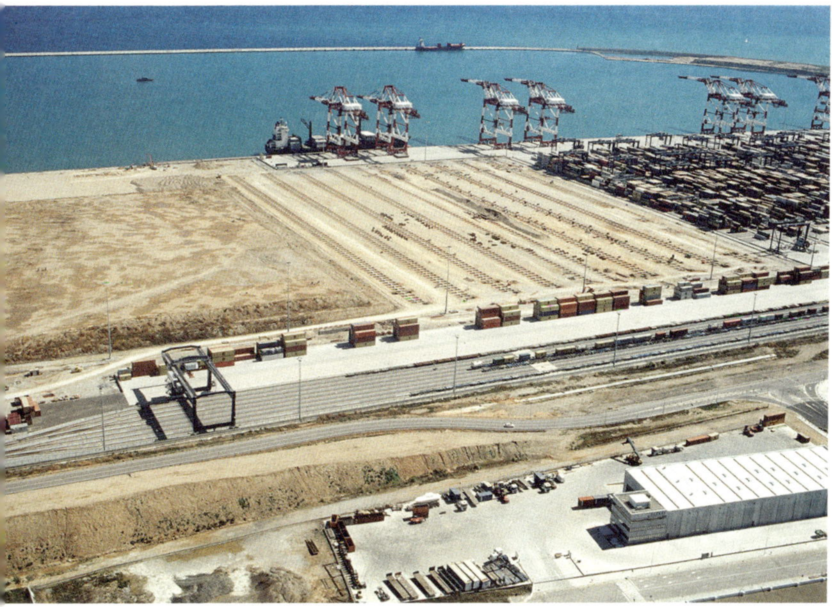

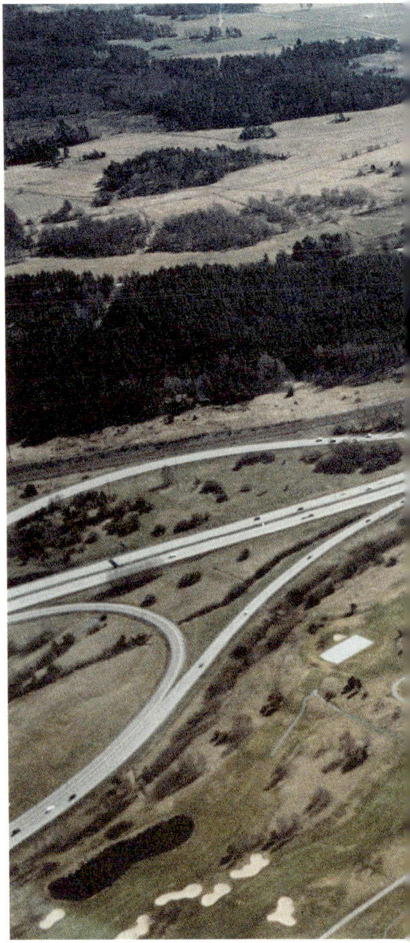

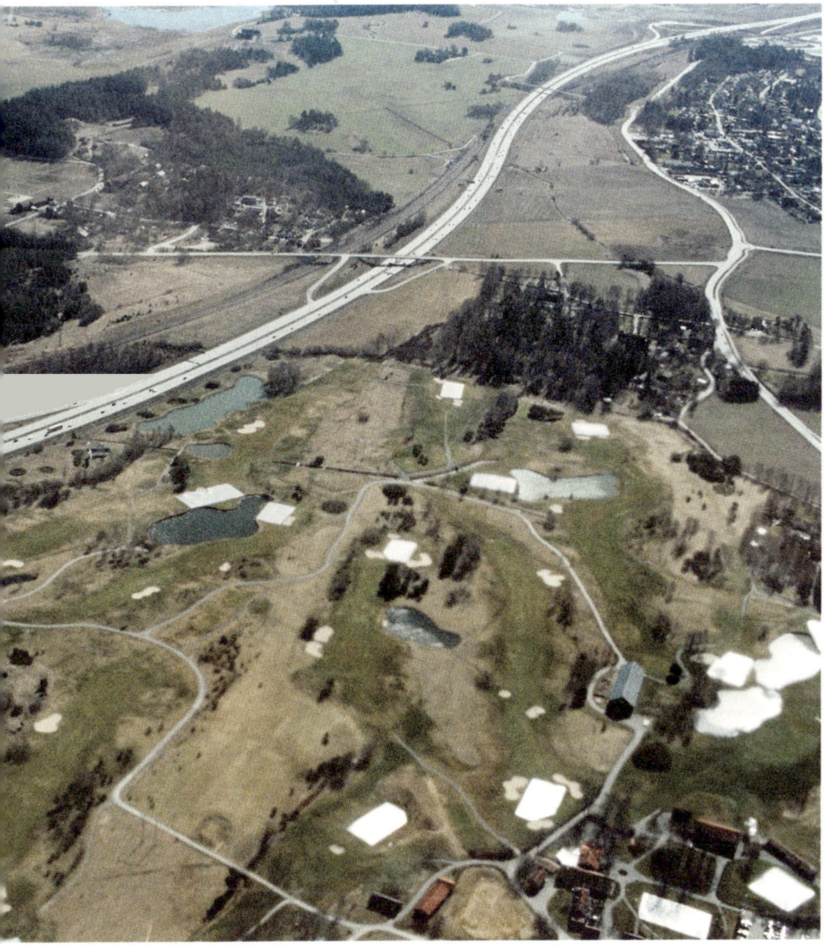

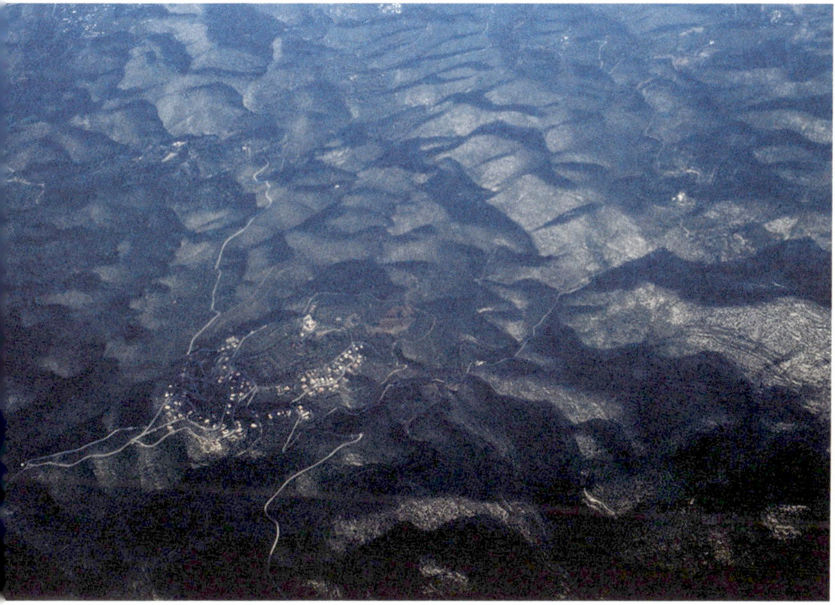

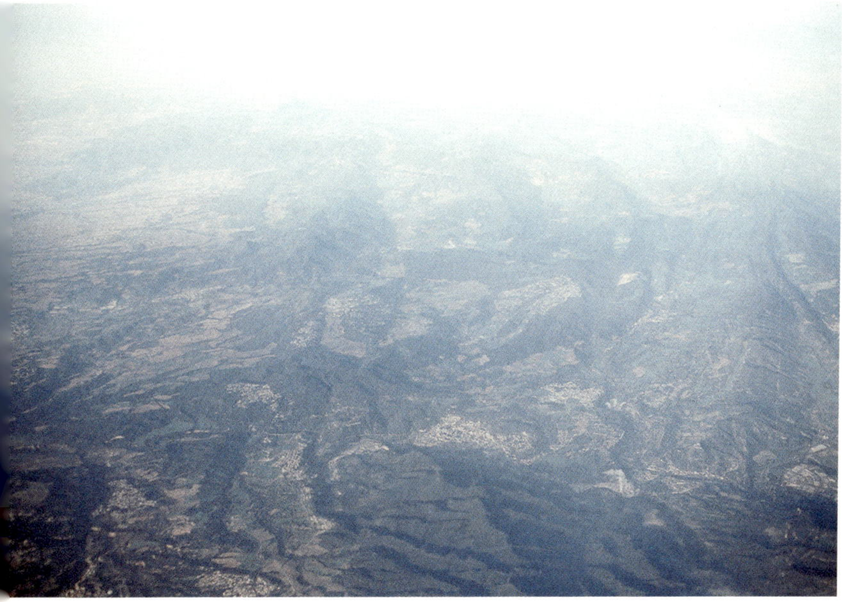

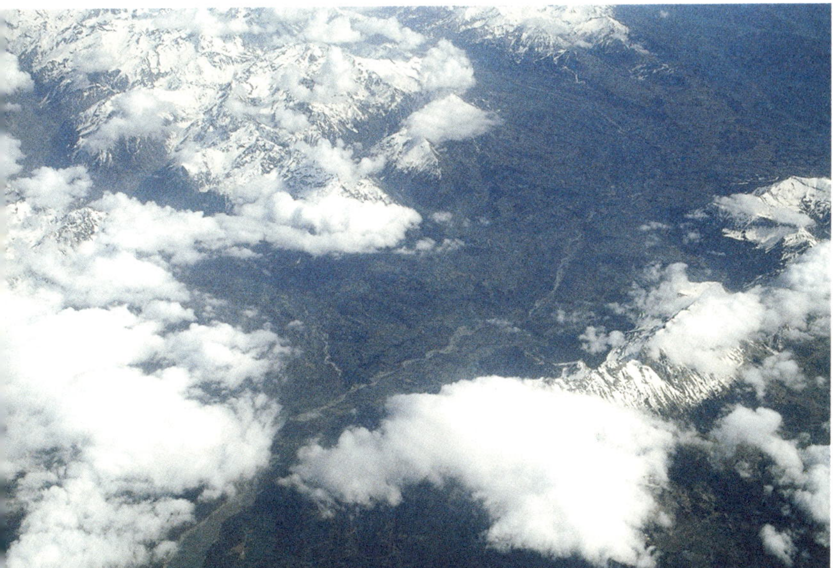

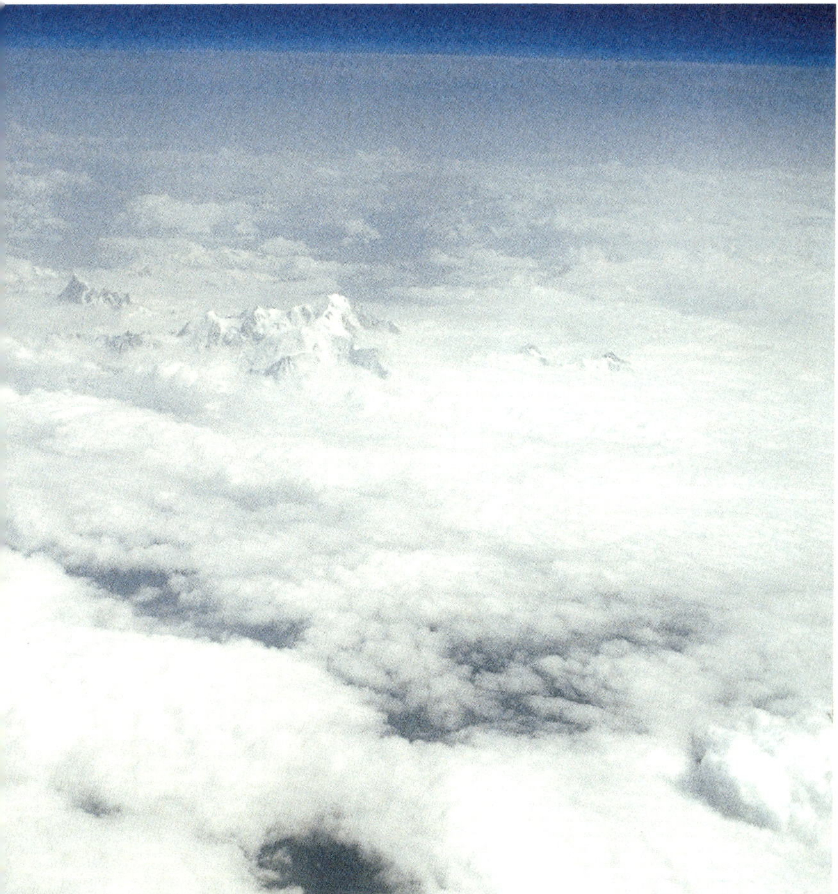

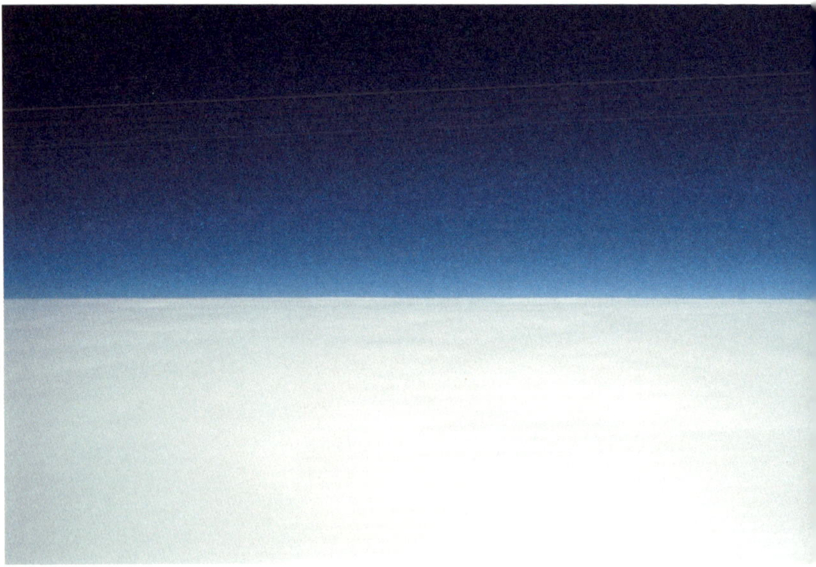

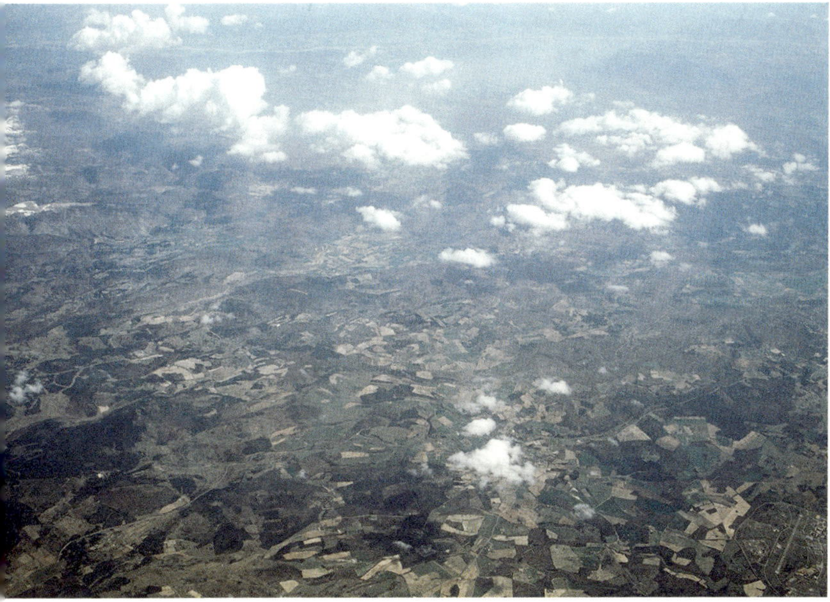

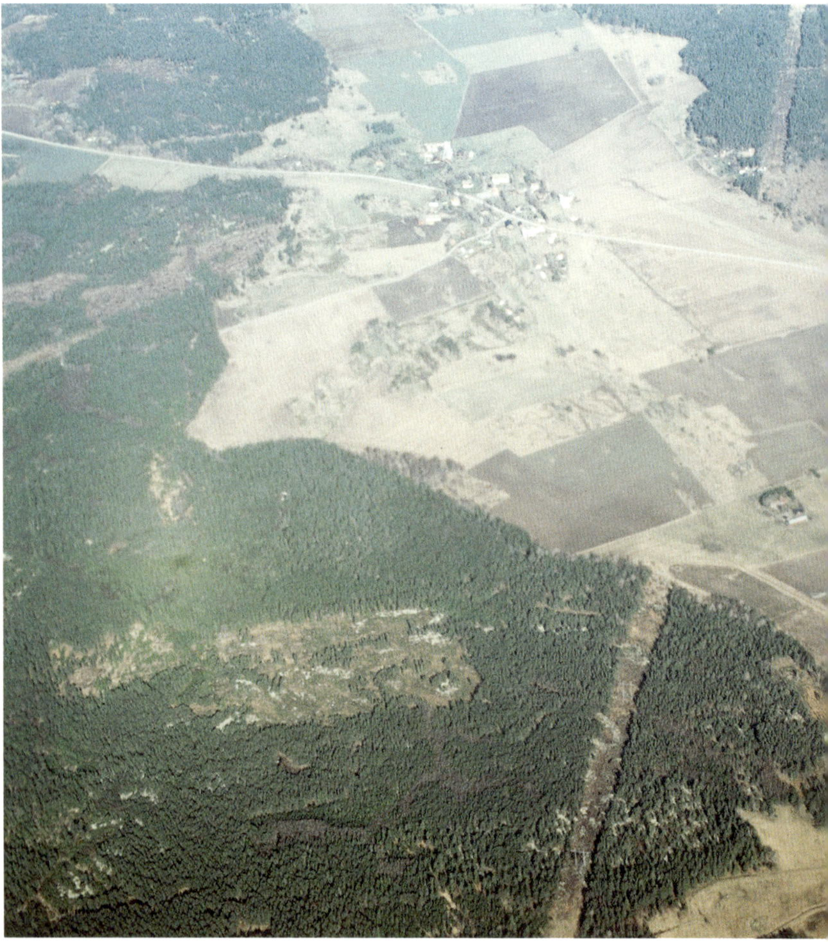

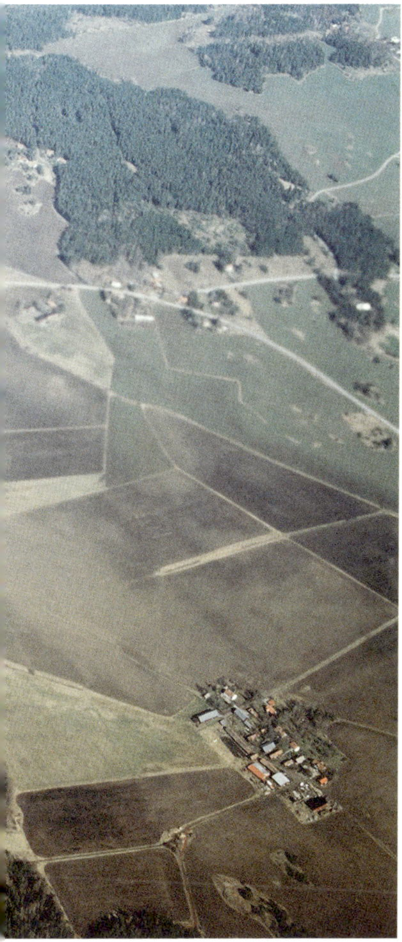

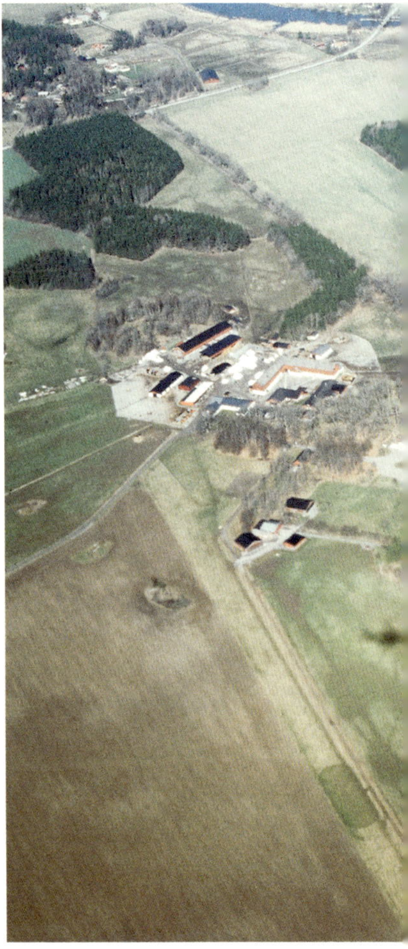

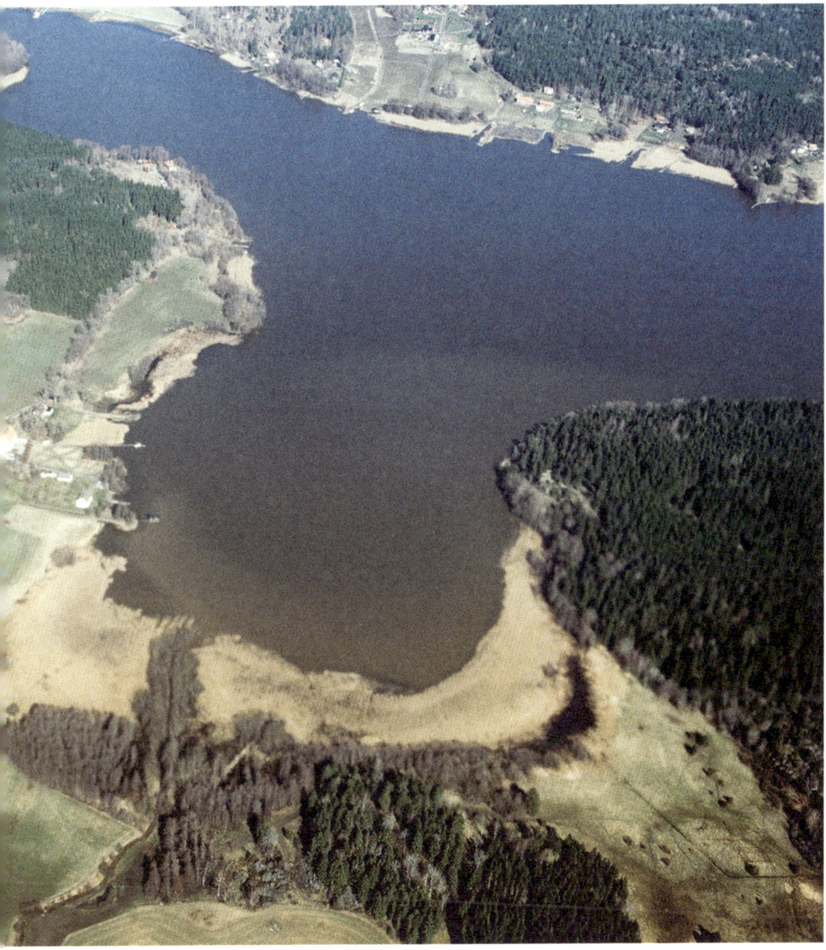

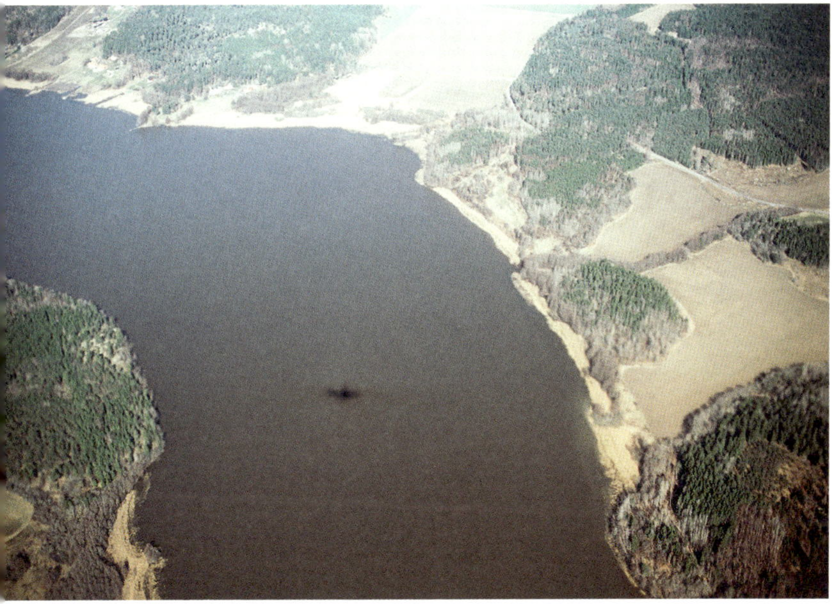

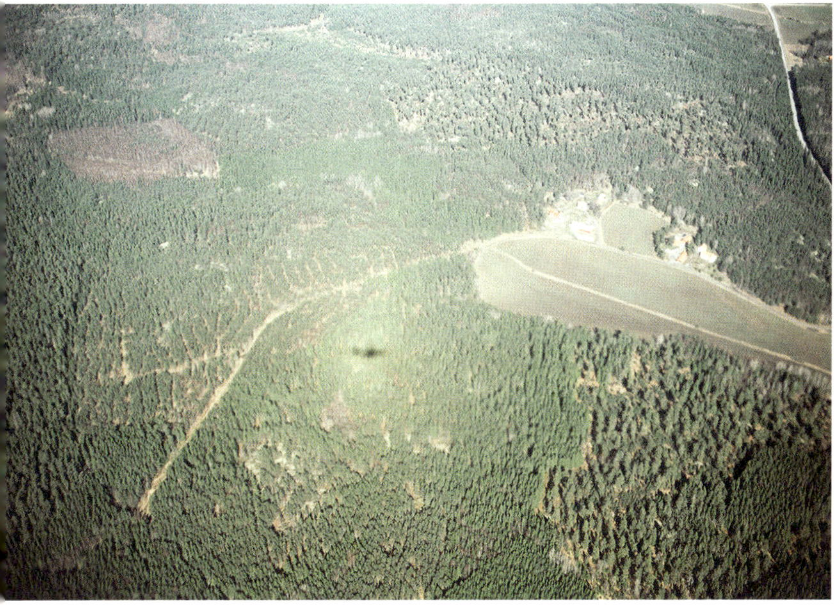

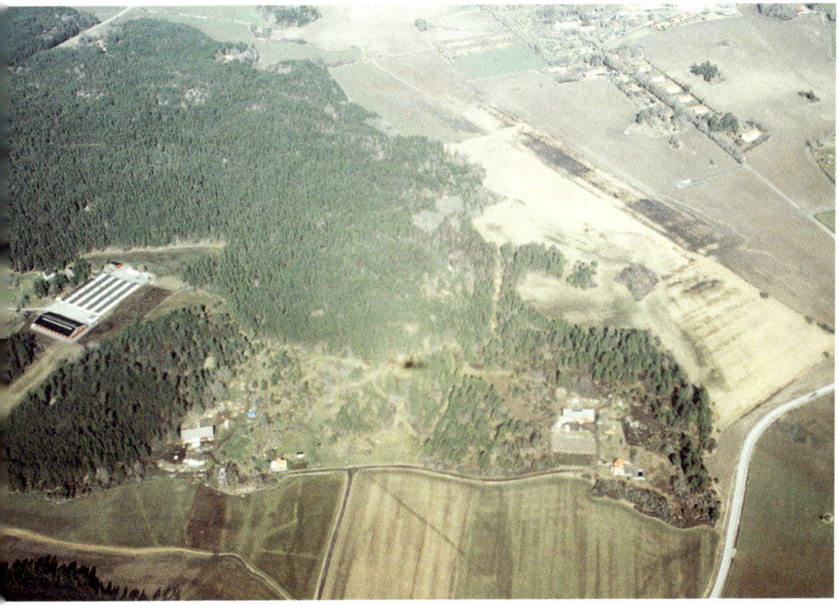

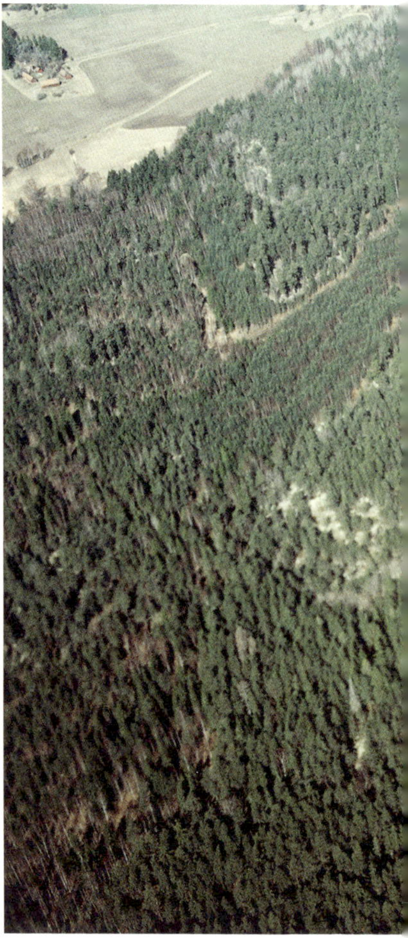

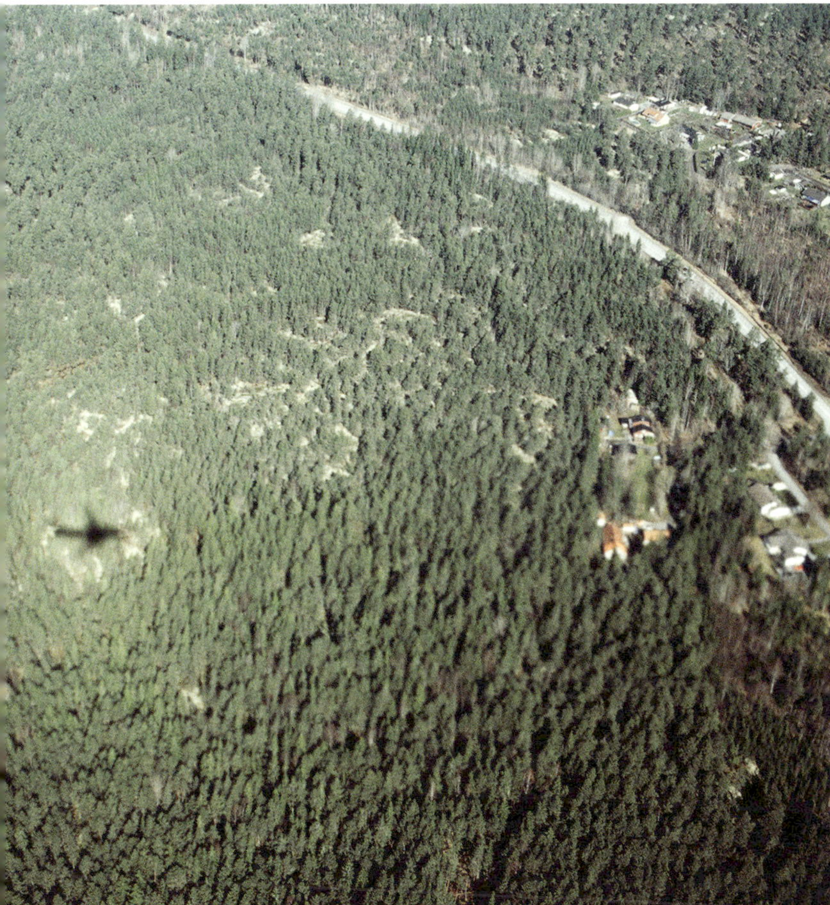

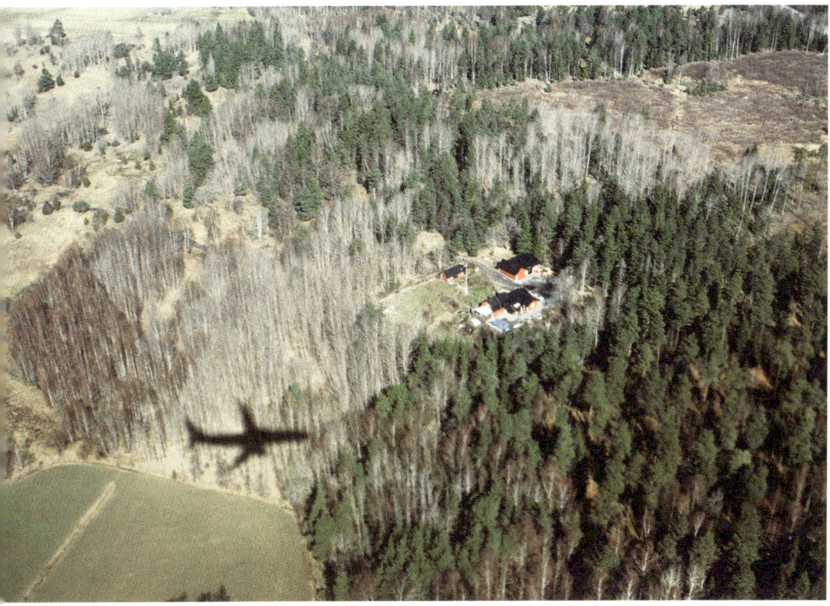

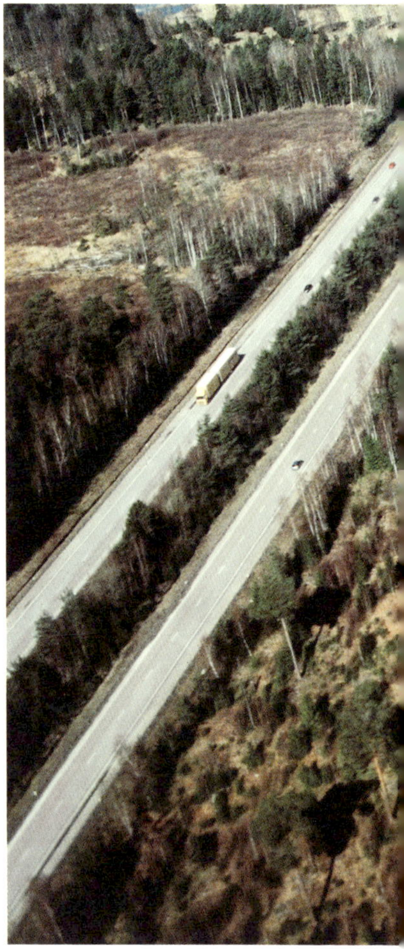

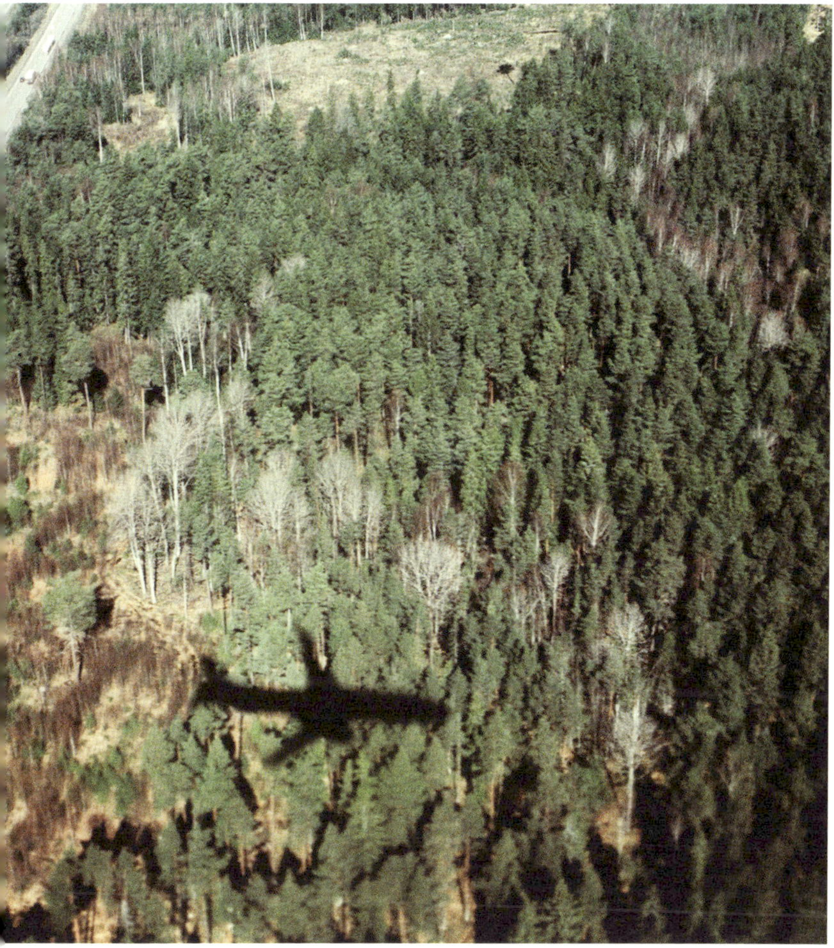

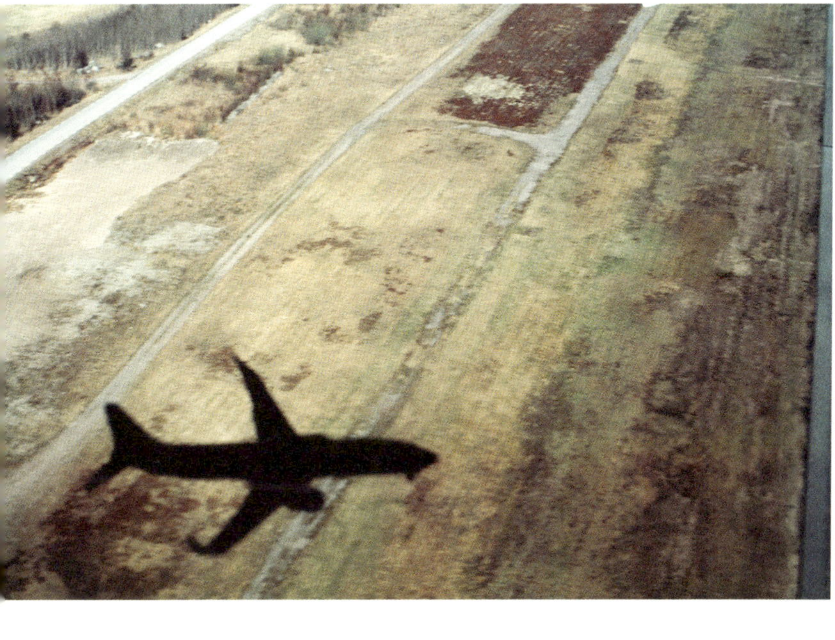

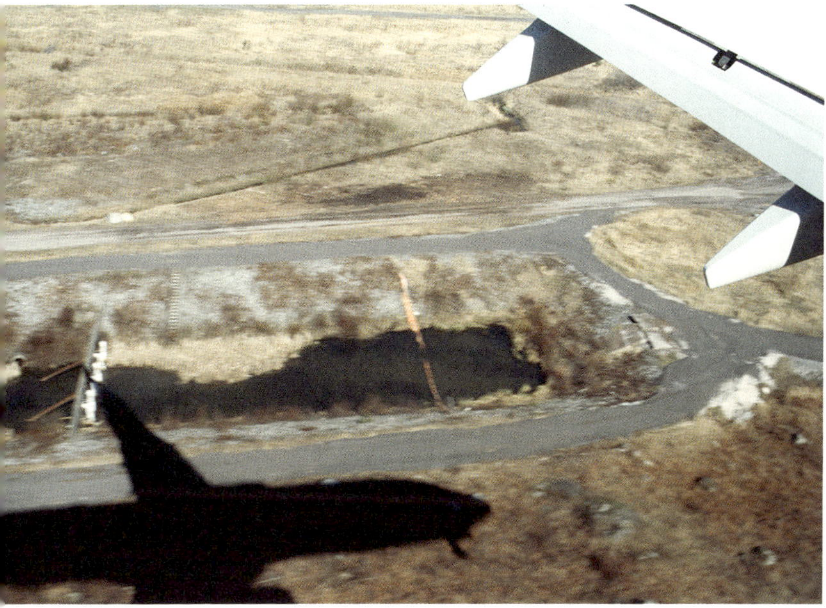

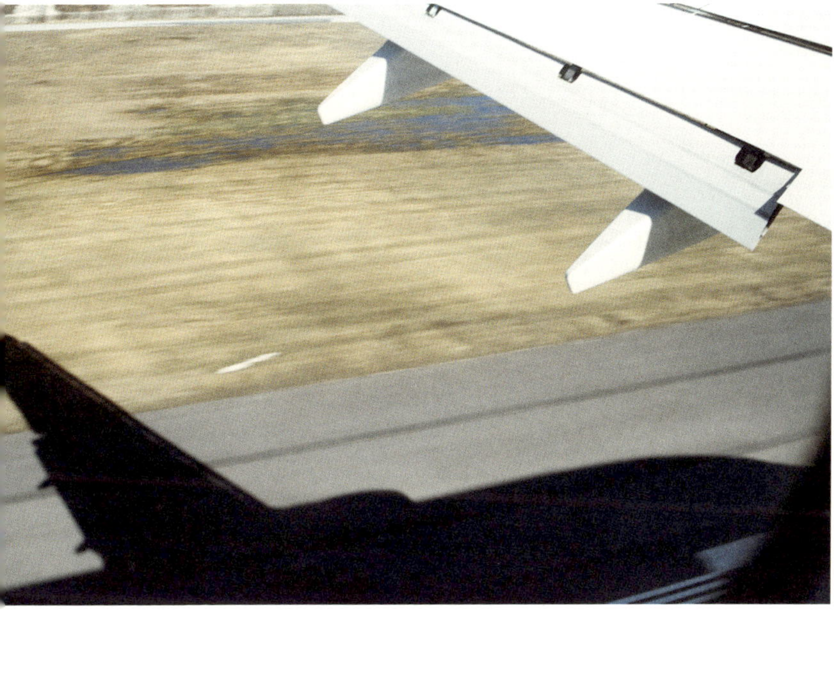

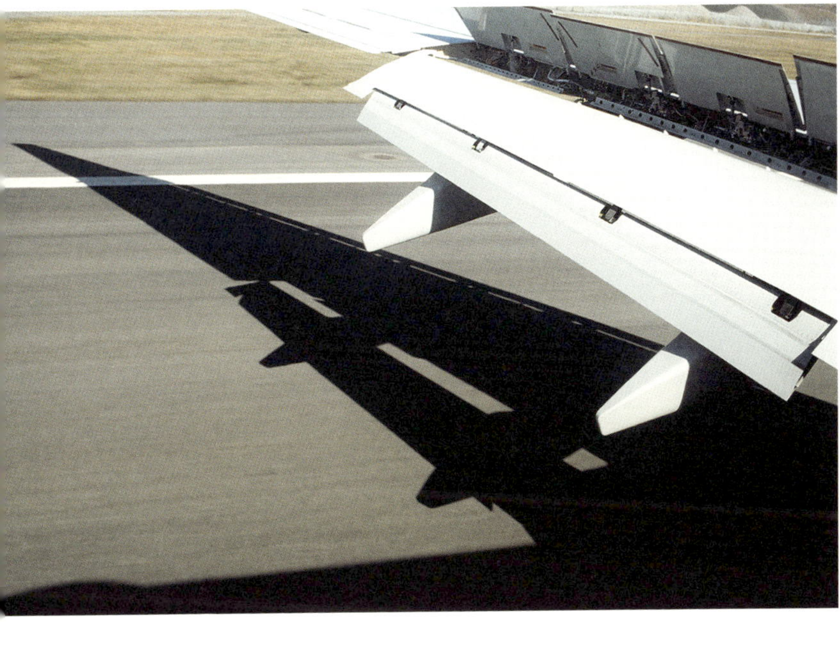

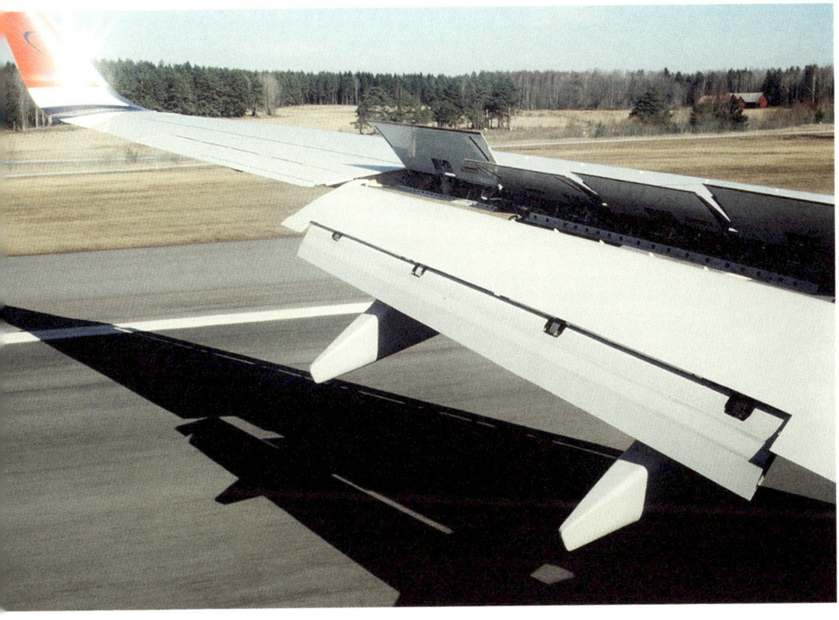

Notes

0 Maurice Blanchot: *The Unavowable Community,* Station Hill Press 1988 New York US, p. 19-20 (*La communauté inavouable,* Les Editions de Minuit 1983)

1 *I*

2 *I*

3 *see*

4 *I*

5 *have*

6 *words*

7 *that*

8 *ring*

9 *out*

10 *the*

11 *chaos*

12 *in me.*

13 *Endless particularity*

14 Maurice Merleau-Ponty: *Silmä ja mieli,* Taide 2006 Tallinn EE (*L'Œil et l'esprit,* Gallimard 1964)

15 Gillez Deleuze: *Essays Critical and Clinical,* Verso 1998 UK, p. 34 (*Critique et clinique,* Les Editions de Minuit 1993)

16 Gaston Bachelard: *The Poetics of Space,* Beacon Press 1994 Boston US (*La poétique de l'espace,* Presses Universitaires de France 1958)

Colophon

This project has received support from:
Arts Promotion Centre Finland | Taiteen edistämiskeskus on myöntänyt kirjalle valokuvateosten laatutukea
Konstföreningen i Åbo | Turun Taideyhdistys ry

Copyediting: Nick Triani
Graphic design, layout: Appu Jasu
Project Management Kerber Verlag: Verena Simon
Paper: Munken Pure, 130 g/m²

www.appujasu.com

The Deutsche Nationalbibliothek lists this publication in the Deutsche Nationalbibliografie; detailed bibliographic data are available on the Internet at http://dnb.dnb.de.

Printed and published by:
Kerber Verlag, Bielefeld
Windelsbleicher Str. 166–170
33659 Bielefeld
Germany
Tel. +49 (0) 5 21/9 50 08-10
Fax +49 (0) 5 21/9 50 08-88
info@kerberverlag.com

Kerber, US Distribution
ARTBOOK | D.A.P.
75 Broad Street, Suite 630
New York, NY 10004
T: +1 (212) 627-1999
F: +1 (212) 627-9484

KERBER publications are available in selected bookstores and museum shops worldwide (distributed in Europe, Asia, South and North America).

ISBN 978-3-7356-0505-4
www.kerberverlag.com

Printed in Germany